Red for Remembrance

Red for Remembrance

THE BRITISH LEGION: 1921–1971

by

ANTONY BROWN

Foreword by

**Admiral of the Fleet
The Earl Mountbatten of Burma,**
K.G., P.C., G.C.B., O.M., G.C.S.I.,
G.C.I.E., G.C.V.O., D.S.O., F.R.S.

Dear well done Karen.

Ian May-Loader

MAYOR OF HOVE.

8/5/85.

HEINEMANN : LONDON

William Heinemann Ltd
15 Queen St, Mayfair, London W1X 8BE
LONDON MELBOURNE TORONTO
JOHANNESBURG AUCKLAND

First published 1971
© British Legion 1971
434 08890 0

Printed in Great Britain by
C. Tinling & Co. Ltd, London and Prescot

Foreword

Of the many organizations with which I am connected, I value none more highly than the British Commonwealth Ex-Services League of which I have been the Grand President since 1946. The British Legion is one of the League's senior and most respected members and indeed may be regarded as its father, for just as the Legion was founded by Lord Haig in 1921 to join this country's ex-service organizations into one strong unified body, so the League was founded shortly afterwards with Lord Haig as its first Grand President, to co-ordinate all ex-service organizations throughout the Empire, as it was at that time.

My home town, Romsey in Hampshire, has a special connection with the history of the British Legion for it was here in 1917 that my father-in-law, the late Lord Mount Temple, founded one of the major ex-service groups called 'Comrades of the Great War'. After the famous Unity Conference in May 1921, the Comrades Association gave up their headquarters and merged with other ex-service organizations to form the British Legion but the Romsey Comrades Club still continues to flourish and I am proud to be its President.

When I became Grand President of the British Commonwealth Ex-Services League in 1946 I also accepted Presidency of the Romsey Branch of the British Legion, an office which I am proud to have held for twenty-five years, and I was deeply honoured and touched when, in July 1966, I was presented with the British Legion's Gold Badge by my former colleague in South East Asia and the then President of the Legion, General Sir Oliver Leese.

It is not for these reasons alone I was delighted to accept the invitation to write this foreword. I welcome the publication of this book on the occasion of the Legion's 50th Anniversary for it provides an excellent opportunity to inform a wider public of the magnificent record of this organization which has woven itself into the community life of our cities, towns, and villages.

As its title implies, this book is primarily about Remembrance.

Foreword

Each year on Remembrance Day we keep the two minutes silence, and this ceremony, so impressively carried out, is observed not only at the Cenotaph in Whitehall, but in every corner of the Commonwealth.

However, this book is not merely a call to Remembrance. It reminds the public of the British Legion's unstinting day-to-day work on behalf of the ex-services community. I refer to the respect and the benefits which the ex-service men and women, and particularly the war disabled and widows enjoy today; so different from the treatment accorded our returning ex-servicemen in 1918. This nation owes a great debt to the Legion for the part it has played in helping to forge the Welfare State as we now know it.

Above all, this book not only records the Legion's role in the welfare and social life of the country, it searches into the future role of this great organization and the contribution it can make to the British way of life, and the chapter on the British Commonwealth Ex-Services League tells of the splendid work being done by constituent members of the League for the ex-service men and women in the Commonwealth, thus strengthening the bond of comradeship and friendship between our peoples.

There is a definite need for increased Legion activity in community affairs, particularly in matters pertaining to youth. We have dedicated ourselves to the principles of maintaining democracy and peace, and I am convinced that this progressive national organization, made up from men and women with a high sense of duty and mindful of the opinion of others, will play a major role in maintaining these principles.

The Legion today is as strong as at any time in its history. It needs boldness in the future; it needs the continued infusion of young men and women from our defence forces. If we are to maintain the standards of which we have been so proud in the past, we must retain those qualities of initiative, tenacity, courage, and *esprit de corps* which were so abundant in times of war.

As we in the British Legion take justifiable pride in remembering all that has been achieved in the past, let us not overlook the vital need to think and act constructively about our future.

Mountbatten of Burma

A.F.

Contents

List of Plates

Author's Note

In writing this book I have had two aims. First, to give the ordinary Legion member some account of the story and activities of his organization in this, its Jubilee year; and second, to try to bring some of these activities before a wider public. With these aims in mind, I have sought to give an impression of the Legion's life rather than to write its history. This has been admirably told in Mr Graham Wootton's Official History and I have not attempted to tread the same ground. If there are gaps in my essentially brief summary of the early period, my excuse must be that this has already been so well covered in Mr Wootton's book.

Perhaps the pleasantest part of any author's task is to thank the people who have helped him, and I must first record my appreciation of Earl Mountbatten's kindness in writing the foreword. I would also like to thank the senior officials of the Legion for their unfailing courtesy and help. General Sir Charles Jones, the President, and Mr Dennis Cadman, the National Chairman, have both given much of their time to discussing the future of the Legion with me. To Mr David Coffer, the General Secretary, I owe a special debt for his encouragement and constant readiness to explain the Legion's work from its widest aspects to the smallest detail.

In the earlier historical chapters I have been especially helped by Sir Gordon Larking. Mr Charles Busby has been a mine of information not only about Preston Hall but many other aspects of the Legion. I am most grateful to Lieut.-General Sir Brian Horrocks for reading the Nijmegen war graves chapter in manuscript. I must thank Major John Rivers and his staff, especially Mr Birt, for their endless patience in explaining the subtleties of pensions law and problems; Mr Stedman and Mr Lardent at the Legion Taxi School; Mrs Croft Foulds for telling me about the Women's Section; Squadron-Leader Victor Cox; Air Commodore Brian Roberts of the British Commonwealth League for Ex-Servicemen; Mr and Mrs Peter Vermeeren for their great kindness to me in Holland; Mr Simpson and Mr Mutimer at the Poppy Factory, and Captain Tickner at the Poppy Warehouse; Mr Ron Pennells; Mr Arthur Markham; Mr Etherington at the Cambrian Factory; and Mr Toomey at Crosfield House. Among branches and club secretaries I must especially thank Mr Gardner at Openshaw, Mr Boyd and Mr Shaw at Newton Aycliffe, and Mr Gable at Bethnal Green.

I must also record my thanks to the following publishers for permission to quote copyright material: Earl Haig of Bemersyde, for extracts from Earl Haig's letters; Lord Norwich, for extracts from *Haig* by Duff Cooper, published by Faber and Faber Ltd.; the Hamlyn Publishing Group, for extracts from *The World Crisis* by Winston Churchill, published by Messrs Thornton, Butterworth; Mrs Nicolete Gray and the Society of Authors on behalf of the Laurence Binyon estate, for the verse from Binyon's *For the Fallen*; Weidenfeld and Nicolson Ltd. for an extract from *The Ribbentrop Memoirs*; Hutchinson Ltd. for an extract from *Douglas Haig: The Educated Soldier* by John Terraine; and William Heinemann Ltd. for an extract from *Count Your Blessings* by Sir Brunel Cohen.

A.B.

Prologue

In the entrance of the British Legion headquarters in London there hangs, framed, a small piece of faded paper. It is a copy, in the poet's own handwriting, of the seventh verse of Laurence Binyon's poem *For the Fallen*:

'They shall grow not old as we that are left grow old:
Age shall not weary them, nor the years condemn.
At the going down of the sun and in the morning
We will remember them.'

'We will remember them' – above all it is the last line which expresses the heart of the British Legion. It is not quite all of what the Legion is about, but it is the essence. It is the inspiration of a record of social service unrivalled in this country, of an organization of nearly three-quarters of a million people whose help and influence has spread to many millions beyond them.

Thus the true beginning of the story is remembrance – the remembrance which happens for most of us, once a year, on a Sunday morning in November, the massive, inward tribute of silence from the thousands round the Cenotaph.

For fifty years the British people have honoured their dead in this manner. Over the years there have been some changes. The veterans with their bowler hats and medals have grown older – each year there are less who have been here from the beginning. Our mode of thinking about remembrance may have changed a little. There is more of the sense of dedication to peace. There is less, if indeed there ever was any, of pomp and circumstance.

Yet at its heart the meaning of remembrance does not change, for it is in essence not public, but personal. If you go down to the Field of Remembrance by Westminster Abbey you feel this still more strongly. Here each regiment, corps, and unit has its own plot where anyone can plant a cross and poppy. Not all are inscribed, but most are, by widows, sons or comrades. 'Dear Grandfather', reads one, 'I never knew you but I think of you very often. Love from Margaret.'

Among the regimental crosses are two that are very old – they are some of the original wooden ones used to mark the graves of unknown British soldiers in Flanders. On another cross you may notice a faded red beret whose story is part of the legend of the Field of Remembrance. One day in 1945 a soldier came here who had been at Arnhem. He asked if there was somewhere he could plant a cross in memory of his comrades, but at that time there was no official space for the paratroops. The soldier put his beret on the grass, planted a cross there, and left it.

It has been kept ever since and is placed, each year, on the cross which now marks the Airborne Forces.

As I leave the Field of Remembrance, I remember some words used by someone in a Legion Club in a new town in County Durham. 'The nation remembers one day in November. The Legion remembers all the year round.'

The aim of this book is to tell the story of how the Legion remembers: of how in the 1970s and beyond, remembrance inspires it to help the living.

PART ONE
The First Half-Century

I
A Land for Heroes

To go back fifty years needs a certain adjustment, more so perhaps than a longer period. We can imagine the age of Nelson or of Queen Elizabeth because those ages were so totally different from ours – we make a mental allowance for the difference, and so form a picture of them more easily. But in terms of history, fifty years ago is almost like our own times. The differences are more subtle. They lie not only in what we might call the props and scenery, but in the smaller shifts in social and human attitudes.

Perhaps the most striking difference between the world of 1918 and our own was its innocence. It was a time when people saw things in black and white, not grey. The promises of politicians, for instance, would not be scrutinized with the sophistication, if you like the cynicism, with which even the younger generation scrutinize such things today. The soldiers had gone out from the towns and villages of England to fight in a cause they believed was just, and they had believed that when they came home their country would reward them with justice.

Lloyd George had spoken of 'homes fit for heroes'; he had promised that the slums which disfigured England would be swept away. Because it was an age of innocence, people had believed him. Underlying the innocence was an almost exhausted sense of relief. On the Western Front alone the British Army had suffered two-and-a-half million casualties in dead, wounded, and prisoners. Now at last the terrible total was complete. The long ordeal was over.

'Thank goodness it's all over – now Jack, we can settle down to peace and plenty,' says the girl to the soldier in the Army Club cigarette advertisement of the time. 'Rather, dear old thing,' he replies. 'Give me plenty of Army Club cigs and I'm at peace with the whole bally world.'*

The soldiers had done their part – so had their families at home who had waited. Now it was up to the politicians to make good their promises. Had they done so – had they even remotely been in a position to do so – the story of the British Legion would have been much more modest. No doubt there would have been some kind of old comrades' association, formed in the spirit of a band of brothers with a common experience.

But because Britain after the war and in the early 1920s was very unlike a land fit for heroes, the British Legion became something different. To begin with it was simply the collective voice of the returned ex-servicemen. Over the years it would become a social force developing with changing times. It would become a society existing for the good of many million people, each one of whom it would see as an individual.

.   .   .   .   .

In one sense the idea of justice for the soldier home from the wars was a new one – till now, ex-soldiers had been treated as somehow expendable. 'Coming the old soldier' was a phrase in vogue as recently as the 1920s, as a description of a crafty or subtle means of scrounging:

* GRAVES, R. and HODGE, A.: *The Long Weekend* (Faber and Faber, 1940), p. 23.

4

the archetypal character of the Military Beggar, as described by Mayhew in his survey of the Victorian poor, still held. He had, said Mayhew:

'All the evidence of drill and barrack life about him, the spare habit, regulation whisker, stiff chin, and deeply-marked line from ear to ear. Ragged though he be, there is a certain smartness about him, observable in the polish of his boots, the cock of his hat, and the disposition of the leather strap under his lower lip.

'If my readers would inquire why a man ready to work should not be able to obtain employment, he will receive the answer that universally applies to all questions of hardship among the humbler classes – the vice of the discharged soldier is intemperance.'*

Thus in Victorian, even Edwardian times, those less compassionate than Mayhew had salved their consciences. The ex-soldier was almost certain a drunk, quite probably a liar who had never been near Ladysmith or Balaclava.

Only now, in 1918, such rationalizations did not work. Britain's army in France had been a people's army. Hardly a family in the length and breadth of the land had remained untouched by the four years' agony of the trenches. When they at last came home the men of that people's army had been promised homes, work, and opportunities.

In the end they too, did not get the things they had been promised as of right. They had to fight for them. The story of their fight is the essential story of the British Legion.

.   .   .   .   .

* MAYHEW, Henry: *London's Underworld*, edited by Peter Quennell (William Kimber, 1950), p. 382.

'There wouldn't have been any British Legion if it hadn't been for Haig.' The view of Sir Gordon Larking, one of the Legion's founder members, is supported by history. Even so, to a later age the figure of the Commander-in-Chief has often seemed somewhat aloof. Compared with the commanders of the Second World War there is no doubt that Haig was a remote figure from his troops. Yet a fairer verdict on the man himself would be that Douglas Haig's native Scottish shyness made it hard for him to show his true feelings. Once when he was visiting a military hospital in Oxford, it was thought that his manner with the wounded soldiers had been abrupt – so much so that an old friend suggested he could have been more forthcoming. It was only then, records Duff Cooper in his biography, that Haig admitted that the meeting had caused him such emotion he had feared that if he said more he would break down.

Almost more revealing was the anecdote of his visit to Lord Haldane after the Victory March in July 1919. Despite being ill with a high temperature, Haig had insisted on riding at the head of his troops in the March. Afterwards instead of going back to bed, as he had promised his doctors, he walked round to one of the houses in Queen's Gate. At the beginning of the war Haig had worked closely with Haldane, then Secretary of State for War, on the creation of Britain's new army. Later Haldane had been hounded from the war ministry, because he had been so rash as to state in public that there were things for which he admired the German nation.

Now, in the hour of triumph, Haig characteristically remembered the man who had helped to shape the victory and now was alone and forgotten. As Haldane watched the crowd dispersing after the March, he was surprised when his servant came up to say there was an officer in uniform to see him, who would not give his name.

Haldane told his servant to show the officer up – when he came into the room, it was Haig. Abrupt and austere as ever, he stayed only a few moments. As he went he left on the table the gift of his recently published War Despatches. Only when he had gone did Haldane open the volume and read the inscription: 'To the greatest Secretary of State for War England ever had.'

Just as he was deeply sensitive to the feelings of a lonely man he honoured, so Haig from the end of the war saw it as his duty to establish the basic rights of the men who had been under his command. At the Armistice he had been offered a viscounty and refused, says Duff Cooper,

'because he had made up his mind that he would accept nothing until he was satisfied that adequate provision had been made for the men and officers who had served under him. When the offer was increased to an earldom he refused it again, and only gave way when it was pointed out to him that all the other recipients of war honours were about to receive them and that it would be difficult to explain why his name alone was omitted. He therefore accepted because he had no wish to make himself unnecessarily conspicuous, to render the position of others uncomfortable or to court an easy popularity.'*

Haig's concern for the welfare of returning soldiers had, in fact, been shown much earlier. In February 1917, in the pause before the final battle of that summer, he had

* COOPER, Duff: *Haig* (Faber and Faber, 1936), vol. II, pp. 410–11.

written to the War Office outlining what he regarded as the minimum standard for the welfare of wounded officers.

'I receive constant communications from private individuals representing the state of poverty and almost destitution to which many of our invalided wounded officers are reduced. A number of them, without any private means of their own, totally and permanently incapacitated by the nature of their wounds from earning a livelihood, are in receipt of a pension which is not sufficient to keep body and soul together, much less to afford them the small comforts which their physical infirmities demand and that their sacrifices in the service of their country have earned.

'In order to deal with these sad and deserving cases, I should suggest that a special Government Department be formed, which should with tact and discretion devote its energies to the interests of the disabled officer.'*

Haig went on to summarize five points which included a proper system of pensions, medical benefit, and welfare for all disabled officers:

'I strongly urge that there should be no delay in dealing with this matter, which, if allowed to continue, will constitute a scandal of the greatest magnitude.'†

When Winston Churchill became Secretary of State for War in January 1919 he found this memorandum shelved, almost unread. All the same Haig's work had not been completely wasted. His basic principles, though in

* Cooper, Duff: ibid., p. 408.
†.Cooper, Duff: ibid., pp. 409–10.

this case only for officers, were in a sense to become the guideline for the British Legion in the future.

. . . . .

In those early days of 1919, however, the formation of a combined ex-service organization must have seemed to those who worked for it, still very far off.

Probably the earliest existing ex-service publication dates from March 1919 – the penny *Bulletin* of the National Federation of Discharged and Demobilised Sailors and Soldiers. A claim for war gratuities, it noted, had received an unsatisfactory reply from the Secretary of State, the Rt Hon Winston Churchill. The Lord Kitchener Holiday Home would provide a fortnight's rest and change of air for Federation members at Lowestoft. The Chairman of the London and North Western Railway offered an amnesty to men who had joined the forces without permission, and now generously offered them reinstatement.

Such was the lukewarm comfort to which the survivors of the Somme returned. Hardly surprisingly, some of them saw the necessity of banding together. The Federation was only one of the bodies which existed to serve ex-servicemen's interests. Beside it, there was the National Association of Discharged Sailors and Soldiers, the National Union of Ex-Servicemen, and an ex-officers' association known as The Comrades.

The latter was the main ex-officer group, but there were many other small ones. After the huge casualties in the first years of the war, there had been frequent promotions from the ranks – thus the new kind of post-1916 officer was often a very different person from his predecessors. He had no private income – the chances were that he came from the middle, not infrequently from the working-class. With demobilization many of these former officers found themselves worse off than the men they had commanded. Unemployed ex-soldiers received a minimal unemployment benefit, but this was for those who had served in the ranks only. Recalls one former official of the later-formed Officers' Association:

'In the early days after the war it was quite a common sight to see a destitute ex-officer playing a barrel organ in the West End, usually with a placard saying he was unemployed and had a wife and children to support. The favourite places were the side-streets beside Selfridges. Here he would get the benefit of large numbers of people passing. If he'd set up his barrel organ in Oxford Street itself, the police would have moved him on.'

Even leaving aside the smaller officers' societies, the existence of the various rival groups may seem at this distance of time, fairly pointless. But if the multiplicity of organizations confuses us, there was at the time another factor. The ex-service movement seemed to contain the seeds of faction – when soldiers had fought alongside each other in France, why should there be one organization for officers and another for men?

There was also a danger of political division. The National Union of Ex-Servicemen, for example, had links with the Labour Party. The Federation had a Liberal M.P., J. M. Hogge, as President, and was in fact regarded as too politically-minded by the Association. 'The Comrades,' wrote T. F. Lister, Chairman of the Federation, 'regarded the Federation as too political, but this did not impress the Federation very much, because there were politicians associated with the Comrades, and the Federation felt that their aim was to stifle criticism of the Government.'

Such divisions seemed counter to everything which wartime comradeship had meant. 'Really,' wrote Haig in a letter to Colonel Crosfield, later the first Vice-Chairman of the British Legion, 'There *ought* to be no question of "rank" in the Legion – we are all comrades.'*

. . . . .

Apart from disunity, the ex-servicemen's organizations had begun to suffer other troubles. When the guns had been silenced on 11 November 1918, the mere absence of war had seemed, in itself, a kind of total perfection. By now the initial optimism had begun to wear off. The returning soldiers began to find that even peace had its minor irritants, and chief among these was the steadily developing row over what were called 'key men'. The story of it has been told at length by Winston Churchill in *The World Crisis* – beginning at the point when on 15 January 1919 he was appointed War Minister and became, as he says, 'immediately confronted with conditions of critical emergency'.

The essence of the key men scheme was that it should make possible the speedier demobilization of men needed to get British industry going rapidly. Prepared by civil servants rather than soldiers, the scheme had already incurred Sir Douglas Haig's disapproval as 'most objectionable and prejudicial to discipline'. Once again, one might feel, Haig's stiffness of speech did not do his feelings justice. What he meant, and certainly what the soldiers felt, was that the scheme was unfair.

* COOPER, Duff: ibid., vol. II, p. 426.

The point about the release of key men was that in many cases it was a question of last in, first out. Many of these particular men had been vital to industry at home, and had not been actually enlisted till the army's almost desperate crisis of manpower in March 1918. Worse still, in Winston Churchill's view, was that many were able to join the ranks of the key men by influence. A letter from an employer at home might often be enough to secure a man's release after only a few months of service – while those who had endured four years of trench warfare found themselves having to stay on.

Apart from the mounting feelings over key men, there were also complaints about bad food and bad accommodation – Churchill, on his arrival at the War Office, found himself faced with a situation of near mutiny. At the Kempton Park depot of the Army Service Corps, the men set up a soldiers' council, marched into Brighton in a show of solidarity with the workers, and lodged a protest with the Mayor. At Luton the Town Hall was burnt by the mob. In Glasgow and Belfast, two brigades had to be brought in to deal with army rioters.

It was perhaps as well for Britain that the man called on to handle the situation understood so instinctively its cause. In *The World Crisis* Churchill has summarized what had led up to it.

'Armies of nearly four million men had been suddenly and consciously released from the iron discipline of war, from the inexorable compulsions of what they believed to be a righteous cause. All these vast numbers had been taught for years how to kill; how to punch a bayonet into the vital organs; how to smash the brains out with a mace: how to make and throw bombs as if they were no more than snowballs. All of them had been through a mill of prolonged inconceivable pressures . . . If these armies were seduced from the standards of duty and patriotism, there was no power which could even have attempted to withstand them.'*

By far the most serious situation arose in France itself, at Calais. On 27 January units of the Royal Army Ordnance Corps and Motor Transport, refused to obey orders. They met the leave boats coming from Folkestone and persuaded the returning soldiers to join them. In a day, a small group of politically active ring-leaders had assumed the command of nearly four thousand men and had, to all intents and purposes, taken over Calais.

Churchill acted swiftly. He recalled two divisions from Germany and put them under the command of General Byng. Significantly, the men under this command had seen action, while most of the ringleaders of the Calais revolt had not. By the night of 29 January the Calais men found themselves surrounded by troops armed with bayonets and machine-guns – and who, moreover, were by now indignant that demobilization might in any way be held back by men who had, to quote Churchill's words, 'in no wise borne the brunt of the fighting'.

At dawn next morning Byng's troops advanced. Unarmed officers called on the rebels to resume their duties. Though the leaders stood their ground, most of their supporters drifted back. So the incident was over without bloodshed.

Nevertheless, revolt on this scale was ominous. A

* CHURCHILL, Winston S.: *The World Crisis: The Aftermath* (Butterworth, 1929), p. 60.

further incident, this time in London itself, shows the kind of administrative pinpricks which goaded the soldiers to act against what seemed injustice. On 8 February 3,000 soldiers, mostly returning from leave in the north of England, had gathered at Victoria Station to catch the early morning boat train. The arrangements made by Movement Control were entirely inadequate. The trains were late. Most of the soldiers had spent a cold night on the platform without even a cup of tea. Added to the sense of injustice that they were returning to duty while other men were being released, their feelings had kindled to the point of explosion. They had marched to Whitehall and by the early morning had converged on the Horse Guards building, where they proceeded to lay down their demands to the Staff of the London Command.

Churchill, summoned to the War Office at 8.30 in the morning, made the critical decision – the 3,000 rebels were to be surrounded, disarmed, and arrested.

'I remained in my room, a prey to anxiety. Ten minutes passed slowly. From my window I could see the Life Guards on duty in Whitehall closing the gates and doors of the archway.'*

Another ten minutes went by, then Churchill received a message from the General commanding the London District. The Grenadiers and Household Cavalry had surrounded the men who had now been placed under arrest – which in the amiable British way of dealing with mutineers meant they were taken to Wellington Barracks and given a good breakfast.

* CHURCHILL, Winston S.: ibid., p. 63.

Nobody had been hurt, and the punishments later given were nominal.

Churchill himself wrote later that he blamed the administration which had made no change in its routine at the railway stations since the fighting had stopped.

'For years men had gone back punctually and faithfully to danger and death with hardly any officers or organization just as if they were ordinary passengers on an excursion train. Those responsible had not realized that much more careful arrangements were required in the mild reign of Peace.'*

In the military annals of many countries, such mild incidents might well seem marginal. In the story of the immediate post-war years they illustrate something significant. For four years the British soldier had been acclaimed as a hero. He had suffered the unimaginable ordeal of the trenches and been promised, when it was all over, a hero's rewards. Now that it seemed that the rewards were still remote, the conquering hero had the temerity to enquire when they might be forthcoming.

It might be only a cup of tea on Victoria Station or a sense of unfairness about the delays in demobilization. The British serviceman had begun to formulate a new idea – the idea that he had a right to demand justice.

*CHURCHILL, Winston S.: loc. cit. *Ibid*, p. 14.

2
The Queen's Hall Conference

MEANWHILE Haig was still working patiently towards unity. He had been called in by Winston Churchill to help draw up a practical demobilization scheme after the debacles of the previous winter; now, he had dedicated himself to the cause of a single organization. He summed up his aims in a speech when receiving the freedom of Newcastle in July 1919.

'I am particularly anxious to see the spirit of comradeship practically expressed by the establishment of a closer union between the different ex-servicemen's societies. These private organizations have done already most excellent work. I am most anxious that all that good work should not be spoiled by a development of a line of political cleavage between the great ex-service organizations now existing. I can think of no more unfortunate development of a movement which in its origin and inspiration is so wholly admirable. So I do most earnestly beg of the men who are today in control of the different ex-servicemen's organizations to try and get together, and to endeavour to find some means whereby the sense of comradeship that has already helped us so much may be preserved and strengthened among all who served in the Great War.'

The following month Haig made a tentative move towards putting this precept into practice – he persuaded a number of the small-scale Officers' Help Societies to combine. In one sense the new combination could have been seen as a step backwards. It involved, true enough, the formation of a fifth large grouping – the Officers' Association. On the other hand Haig had established the point he sought to make. The ex-service organizations must combine if they were to prosper.

By the summer of 1920 the point had been well taken. In May the annual conference of the Federation voted that discussions should begin with the other organizations. In August a Joint Conference on Unity took place at the Royal United Services Institution in Whitehall. Its proceedings were increasingly dominated by the six-and-a-half feet tall figure of T. F. Lister, the ex-gunner who until now led the Chairman of the Federation. A committee was set up to form the constitution. Squadron Leader Victor Cox, a representative of the Officers' Association on the committee, has described what its meetings were like.

'Usually we met in a large room at the Royal United Service Institution, the formal meetings being held on average every two months, generally on a Saturday. Most of us were at work through the week and many of us had to travel up from the provinces. As a rule we began at ten in the morning and went on till six o'clock or later.'

Cox himself was a twenty year old ex-airman, who had transferred to the R.F.C. after enlisting in the Welsh Fusiliers at fifteen.

'During the midday break, being embarrassed at the prospect of lunching elsewhere with the Generals, I used to have a sandwich at the public house round the corner. I was the youngest person present by several years, and if I wanted to speak during the meeting I felt a bit shy about it. If that happened, Mr Lister would always help me out. He had a gift for seeing at once the point you were trying to make, and he'd help to make it for you. He had an extraordinary power of persuasion, which made him a brilliant chairman. The other quality I remember was his gentle manner – the way he had of reconciling people. I never knew any conflict of opinion that Mr Lister couldn't settle somehow.'

Another reminiscence of Lister comes from Sir Gordon Larking:

'In those days we were all young men, and we needed someone with a firm hand to guide us. The point about Tom Lister was that he could manage things with a sense of humour but always with a firm hand as well. He also steered us away from the political aspect – if it hadn't been for him we should have been taken over by the Left or the Right. I believe he was a Liberal and had once stood as a Liberal candidate. If he'd been an M.P. he'd have been a first-class one. But it was the Legion's gain that he wasn't.'

Unity for the ex-service organizations may seem to us as simple as it was natural. Even so, it took time before all the obstacles to unity could be overcome. 'I had for some time been convinced,' wrote Lister afterwards, 'that much more was required than the amalgamation of organizations through their executives. It was necessary to devise a scheme which would unite the ex-servicemen as a whole . . . it was therefore a decisive moment, when, in response to my appeal, the Chairman of the Comrades announced that they were agreeable to scrap the whole of their headquarters.'

With unity now clearly in sight, what was to be the name of the new organization? Among forty-nine suggested titles were 'The British Ex-Service Legion', 'The United Services League', 'The Imperial Federation of Comrades'. By the time the first Unity Conference met in May 1921, a simpler, more memorable phrase had been provisionally adopted – the two words, British Legion. 'I think a lot of people quite independently came to the conclusion it was the best name,' said Lister, 'I know I was never attracted by any other title.'

.   .   .   .   .

The Unity Conference at the Queen's Hall was attended by 700 delegates from all over Britain. In one sense its deliberations were only a rubber stamp. The real work of persuasion and discussion had been done in committee during the previous months. But Saturday 14 May 1921 marks the real beginning of the British Legion as a single, unified body. The Prince of Wales, it was announced from the platform had accepted the office of Patron. Earl Haig was elected President in his absence in South Africa, but for the office of chairman there was no need of an election. T. F. Lister's untiring work as a negotiator won him the vote without opposition. Colonel Crosfield was elected Vice-Chairman. The post of Treasurer went to Colonel (later Sir) Brunel Cohen, a legless veteran of Ypres who was later to become the ex-servicemen's firmest supporter in the Commons.

Unity had not come a moment too soon. The ex-servicemen had put their own house in order, but meanwhile the broader world outside was full of confused, sometimes sombre shadows. Certainly by 1921 most people had done their best to forget the war. It was true the newspapers still referred to the Germans as Huns, and the more selfrighteous thundered forth on the necessity of their being made to pay war reparations. Newspaper chauvinism apart, there was little to remind the nation of its debt to the services. The world of 1921 had other things on its mind – cocktails, the foxtrot, the new cult of the flapper, the in-word for the kind of modern young woman who was 'a good sport' and rode pillion on a motorbike.

In the Whitehall clubs and the press the campaign against the now tiring war leader, Lloyd George, began to gather force. There was discontent about the waste of men and money involved in garrisoning the former Turkish province of Mesopotamia. When the post-war industrial boom broke in 1921 the name was adapted as a kind of double taunt to Lloyd George, Mess-up-at-home-here.*

The newspapers began to talk of trade depression – the national figures for unemployment were creeping ominously high. In the coalmines in particular, a brooding discontent was spreading. The miners had hoped to get the owners to adopt a scheme of uniform wages, so that low wages in the poorer pits would be helped out by higher production in the richer ones. The mine-owners had refused and in April 1921 the pitmen came out on strike, supported by the railwaymen and transport workers.

In the end the government approved a yearly subsidy of £10 million to increase wages in the poorer districts,

* GRAVES, R. and HODGE, A.: *The Long Weekend* (Faber and Faber, 1940), p. 70.

and the men went back. All the same the strike had been the first rumbling of industrial dissatisfaction. 'With a continuance of the present industrial strife,' wrote Earl Haig in the first number of the new British Legion *Journal*,* 'there must be an increase of unemployment. The payment of doles under the title of Unemployment Benefit demoralizes the ex-serviceman, and is a suicidal policy which cannot go on indefinitely.'

Such grave reminders apart, the first issue of the new *Journal* was an occasion for congratulation. It began with a specially written poem by Thomas Hardy entitled *A Call to National Service*. Though even here the first line and title, in view of the impending unemployment situation, must have seemed faintly ironic:

'Up and be doing, all who have a hand
To lift, a back to bend. It must not be
In times like these that vaguely linger we
To air our vaunts and hopes; and leave our land.
Untended as a wild of weeds and sand.
– Say, then, 'I come!' and go, O women and men
Of palace, ploughshare, easel, counter, pen;
That scareless, scathless, England still may stand.

Would years but let me stir as once I stirred
At many a dawn to take the forward track,
And with a stride plunged on to enterprise,

I now would speed like yester wind that whirred
Through yielding pines; and serve with never a slack,
So loud for promptness all around outcries!'

* The name *Journal* was not in fact used immediately: the first few numbers of the paper were issued under the title 'British Legion'. For simplicity's sake, I have called it the *Journal* for these earlier years as well.

There were also cautious good wishes from Lloyd George and rather more enthusiastic ones from such other notabilities as St John Ervine, Sir Hall Caine, and the dramatist Sir Arthur Wing Pinero. (Later issues included material of a slightly less high-toned nature – serials and short stories by Sapper, Edgar Wallace, and the naval writer 'Bartimeus', which were possibly more to the taste of the general reader.) A prize of £5 was offered in a competition to guess the total possible strength of the Legion if all ex-servicemen joined it. A cartoon showed first the British lion chasing off the Kaiser, then in its second picture a stout businessman walking up to a factory where the signboard reads 'closed – owing to German competition'. In the later pages an anonymous writer began a series of articles called *Careers for ex-servicemen*, with the *Movie Industry:*

'In common with other professions and trades the cinematograph industry is feeling very acutely the effects of the present slump. Nevertheless, we shall see a great bid for the supremacy of the world in picture producing. There is not the slightest doubt in my mind that the present lead held by America will be gained by us.'

On the same page, more ominously, the Wallace Attwood Efficiency Service invited Legion members in receipt of disability pensions to take up 'Outdoor Selling as a Career'.

That was in July 1921. The following January, the unemployment figures reached two million.

3
'Nothin' doin', lad'

MORE than a quarter of these, the Legion estimated, were ex-servicemen. In the worst hit areas like the north-east, Legion relief committees worked overtime helping the families of servicemen whose children were literally going barefoot: at Fulham, even a holder of the V.C. was found out of work. Lister asked the Government to make a big public works loan to help what he called 'the army of no occupation'. In the *Journal*, the optimistic articles about prospects in the cinematograph industry were replaced by grimmer notices about how to draw unemployment benefits.

One Legion member, the Reverend David Railton, decided to see for himself the conditions that fellow ex-servicemen found when seeking employment. Wearing cast-off clothing and with a shilling in his pocket, he set off on a tour of the North of England. Later he wrote, under the title of *Nothin' doin', lad*, an account of his travels for the *Journal*.

'The expressions on the face of those on the road were mostly full of helpless pity. I approached numerous people and in each case I asked them to tell me where I could get work. None could tell me; they answered me mostly, as did a young mother, wheeling her children in a pram, "Noa, I'm sorry, but I doan't knaw where ye'll get any." In a well-known market town, after many fruitless efforts, I thought I would try one more private house. There the tide turned. The cook gave me 6d. But to get one hour's work? I thought I had managed it at a certain works. A man, who was at work on a car, said, "Not likely," when I asked if there was anything doing. Then the boss came and he took me aside and explained that they were discharging men. Meanwhile he asked me questions and offered me 3s. to pay my fare to a certain city. When I thanked him and said I'd rather do some work, he replied that he knew that. He had been "down and out" himself, and he knew what it was. He told me to take my fare, adding, "If you strike eggs, send it back." I promised to do so, and kept my word later on.'

For a single man such conditions were bad enough: the Legion's own records reveal the appalling conditions of many ex-service families. One man and his children were found sleeping in orange boxes with leaves as bedding. Another suffering from the psychological illness then known as shell-shock, lived with his family in a bell tent in the woods.

What, in the face of all this, could the Legion do? The immediate answer it gave was far-seeing and practical. A special Employment Committee was set up which gave direction and financial help to Area Councils to handle the problem on a regional basis. Improvised work schemes were introduced – Colonel Crosfield took 200 men to France to work on the reconstruction of war-shattered railways. Another 220 worked on special ship-breaking schemes at Ramsgate and Plymouth. Other projects included salmon fishing in Southern Ireland, the laying of mosaic floors in banks and public buildings.

Preference was given to ex-servicemen on various local authority schemes. The Legion helped many others to start small businesses. By November 1921 it was reported that the Unity Relief Fund had dealt with 150,000 cases of distress by giving out food vouchers on local tradesmen and meal tickets at various centres. The Legion's Women's Section, set up in the same year as the Legion itself, organized relief centres and provided emergency food and clothing. 'Most dreadful is it to think,' said *The Times*, 'what the case would be but for the work of the British Legion.'

But if rising unemployment was a threat to the service-man who had come safely through in 1918, it was many times worse for the disabled. Long before the formation of the Legion itself, the National Federation had tried to get some sort of scheme going whereby employers would be compelled to take on a quota of disabled men. The leaders of the Federation had met Lloyd George, who had given a deft politician's answer to Lister:

'The proposal regarding compulsion requires very careful consideration. It affects not only the employers, but it affects the trade unions, and it affects also the workers. A man who is forced into a works, and has thereby a statutory right, is not always very helpful. It would be dangerous to the man himself . . .'

In other words the implication of compulsion would also be the universally disliked principle of the compulsion of labour. The Federation's high hopes had foundered on a shrewdly-made debating point.

A less political view of the case against compulsion came from George Bernard Shaw, an unexpected contributor to the *Journal*:

'The policy of Mr Tupman, who was indefatigable in his efforts to help the poor by asking other people to give them cast-off clothes and jobs, seems cheap; but it is no use on a national scale. No man in his senses will employ a disabled man when he can find a sound one; and the talk about compulsion is silly. Disabled men drag down wages and standards of work. They should not be employed at all industrially. The duty of the country is perfectly clear. These men were disabled in its service, and should be supported by it unconditionally.'

Which would have been all very well, one is tempted to add, if there had been the slightest sign of the Government acting in the spirit of Shaw's last sentence. So far the most practical scheme they had produced was what was known as the King's National Roll Scheme. Under this, employers were encouraged to take on at least a proportion of five per cent disabled men. Those who did so had their names inscribed on the special roll, and were also granted an insignia known as the Seal of Honour, which they could use on letterheads and in advertisements.

The *Journal*, in fact, carried their advertisements on special pages – they ranged from Booths' Mature Dry Gin to Peter Robinson's, from Onoto the Pen to Reudel Bath Saltrates ('For All Foot Troubles'). Even so only a small minority of firms had co-operated: out of 1,182,000 disabled men who came within the provision of the scheme, only 137,000 were on the books. The trouble was that the scheme rested, said the *Journal*, 'entirely upon the power of sentiment – a power which lessens as years dull the memory'.

Even so, the Government continued to refuse the

principle of compulsion. In 1922 the case for it was argued again by the Legion's Assistant Secretary, J. R. Griffin, before a Select Committee, but the Government was unyielding. Recommendations were made to give employers more incentives to take on disabled men. If the voluntary scheme had not proved itself by May 1923, some form of compulsion might be reconsidered.

For the moment it seemed these concessions were the best the ex-servicemen were likely to get. But by now the Legion was getting used to receiving a dusty answer.

.   .   .   .   .

It is worth making one point about the early years of the British Legion – as we follow the often-discouraging single events, we may be in danger of losing the general pattern. In the 1920s especially the Legion was often engaged in a series of holding or defensive actions against a government and a society which was itself facing increasingly darker problems. Against the background of spreading unemployment, strikes, and world depression, the Legion's negotiators must sometimes have looked on their task almost despairingly. Because they did not despair, a later generation was to reap the benefit. Almost every advantage won by the returning soldiers after World War II was an eventual product of the work and devotion of those who had fought the Legion's battles from the beginning.

Nowhere is this principle more valid than in the story of pensions, and there can be few to whom the Legion owes a greater debt than to men like Alex Webb and T. J. Birrell of the pensions department. Laborious, complicated as their task must often have seemed, it is to their eternal credit that they never lost sight of the human distress that lay beneath the detail. Years later, in a very different social climate, almost everything they had fought for would be gained. Not only ex-servicemen, but the whole community, would benefit from their efforts.

.   .   .   .

At the end of the war the pension rate had been fixed at thirty shillings a week for a man who was totally disabled – but apart from the flat rate, the Legion's wider concern was to get the whole system of pensions revised and reconsidered. Till now the law had been that if an ex-serviceman became ill, it was up to him to prove that it was a result of war service. Consistently the Legion tried to get this law reversed – to put the onus in effect on the Government, to prove that incapacity or illness was *not* the result of his war service. The other basic principle of the pensions system which the Legion wanted to change was the seven year limit, under which a man could not claim a pension more than seven years after the time of his discharge.

Close in-fighting with the Government on all these issues went on through the 1920s. It went on in Parliament, in the lobbies, and in some less exalted places as well. Sir Gordon Larking, in those days a young ex-soldier, recalls how he often spoke from a soapbox in Maidstone:

'The Pensions Minister in those days was named Tryon – Try-on, I used to call him in my speeches. You couldn't believe the way they refused pensions even when they were badly needed. I remember one chap who came to us for help. A great big chap he was, but he'd got a wound in the leg. When he went to the Pensions Office they wouldn't look at him. "A big chap like you," they used to say, "what do you want a pension for?" '

Partly, says Sir Gordon, such attitudes stemmed from the fact that few of the civil servants in the Ministry of Pensions had been in the army:

'They were all Treasury men, so naturally if anyone came and asked them for money their reaction was how they could defeat it. Later, after the second war, all this was different – all the senior men in the Ministry were ex-servicemen and they understood the problem.'

Meanwhile in Parliament, the Legion's main voice continued to be Brunel Cohen, who in 1925 presented what probably remains the longest petition addressed to the House of Commons in this century:

'The number of signatories which the Legion had collected totalled 824,105. At that time a man was not entitled to a pension unless his disability proclaimed itself within seven years, and, as in many cases illnesses and sickness directly due to war service took longer than that to develop, it was considered extremely unfair that a claim should be ruled out entirely on an arbitrary time limit. Papers had been signed by hundreds of thousands of people throughout the country and bundles were delivered by van at the House early one afternoon. I then had to rise in my seat and announce to the Speaker that I wished to present this petition. He instructed me to bring it to him and I recollect that I took one sheet in my hand, the remaining scores of very large bundles being taken round to the back of his Chair and, I believe, deposited in sacks.'*

Predictably the Petition did not achieve its main object. It did, however, help to secure one small point – and incidentally to illustrate what the *Journal* called 'the wonderful subtlety of politicians' minds'. When the Minister rose after the presentation he made no announcement on the subject, but seized the opportunity of saying that pensions would be fixed till 1929. There would be no cuts, at least, in the immediate future.

* COHEN, Brunel: *Count Your Blessings* (William Heineman, 1956), p. 67.

4
The Hand of Friendship

MEANWHILE 824,105 signatures on the National Petition were an indication of the new and growing strength of the Legion. By the mid-1920s it had become completely accepted as part of the fabric of British life – there were now 2,500 branches and 145,000 members. At Whitsun 1925, the fourth anniversary of the Unity Conference, the Legion received its Royal Charter. In the same year the British Legion Village was set up at Preston Hall, near Maidstone, as a self-contained community for ex-service T.B. victims.

After the first Poppy Day in 1921, Major George Howson had set up a small workshop in Bermondsey to employ a handful of disabled men on making poppies. By June 1925, there were 191 workers. To accommodate them, the Poppy Factory now moved from Bermondsey to new premises at Richmond. In the summer of 1925, the Legion's Women's Section began a new scheme for sending children on country holidays – the first item on a programme of social relief which would eventually include convalescent homes, widows' allowances, and the provision of homes and hostels for the children of ex-servicemen.

Soon this diversity would be enriched still further. Since 1919 a small factory in Breconshire had given work to eight disabled men, working on the production of Welsh tweed. In 1927 the whole factory was handed over

to the Legion by its owner. In the same year a grant of
£2,000 was made to a school for training London taxi
drivers – later to become one of the most successful of
all the Legion's ventures.

Thus the pattern of the Legion's work was now emerg-
ing. In the foreground the individual schemes such as the
London Taxi School and Preston Hall – as a perhaps
drabber background, there were the unremitting, often
unrewarding efforts to badger successive Governments
into giving the ex-serviceman a fair deal. Clearly these
forms of social service were the Legion's main functions.
What, meanwhile, were its wider beliefs, the attitudes that
any such organization is bound to have to the world
around it?

From the start, the Legion had been non-political. On
the whole the virtues its members believed in were the
traditional ones of loyalty, comradeship, and duty. Beyond
that the Legion's leaders carefully did not go. The Legion
itself included the supporters of all political parties and
of none. On the ground of self-interest alone, it would
have been the greatest folly for the Legion to be aligned
politically. As John Terraine writes in his biography of
Haig:

> 'Many ex-servicemen's associations in other lands
> have been political instruments, lobbies and pressure
> groups, concerned with battles almost as ferocious as
> those of the wars in which their members fought. The
> British Legion is a splendid exception.'*

As far as domestic politics were concerned, the Legion's
role was thus rightly, indeed inevitably, limited. Looking

---

* TERRAINE, John: *Douglas Haig: The Educated Soldier* (Hutchinson,
1963), p. 484.

further afield, it has had a wider, in some ways a special function. From the beginning the Legion was the mouthpiece of those who had fought for their country in the 1914 war. As such, it was uniquely fitted to make links with similar groups in other countries.

Gradually as the nation settled into peace it seemed natural to make links with the foreign ex-servicemen. In November 1921 the Legion appointed five of its senior officers to F.I.D.A.C., the international ex-servicemen's organization whose initials stood for *Fédération Interalliée des Anciens Combattants*. The operative word was *Interalliée* – interallied – for the first rule of F.I.D.A.C. was that German and other ex-enemy organizations were barred.

To some of the more far seeing Legion delegates, particularly Colonel Crosfield and Brunel Cohen, this view seemed a narrow one. In 1926 the Legion conference passed a resolution urging F.I.D.A.C. to seek new ways of collaboration and understanding with the ex-enemy countries. The following year, after long negotiations of immense complexity, a German and Austrian delegation attended a F.I.D.A.C. conference at Luxemburg. On the first day all seemed to go well. Then came the question of agreeing on the meeting's main resolution: the *Journal* for August 1927, takes up the story:

'On the second and concluding day of the conference, the delegates assembled full of hope and confidence. Whispered warnings that the Germans would prove difficult were not credited.

'The plenary assembly was opened and the main resolution was read and much approved, for it reflected a sincere desire to please. It had been carried when an

Alsatian representative enormous with a shaggy beard and a lame leg, rose to say that he, who spoke and understood German as intimately as he knew French, had noticed that the Germans in their translation of the resolution had so arranged it as to alter completely the sense of the vital clauses which stated that peace must rest on respect for the existing treaties.

'At first it was thought that this was merely a clumsy translation, but presently, when the Germans absolutely refused to alter their text, so as to make this vital point clear, it was realized that a most serious situation had arisen.

'The delegates broke into gesticulating groups, the journalists dashed off to telegraph the news. Everything was confusion. It was remarkable how hard the French tried to meet the Germans. One and all they strove to persuade them to agree. But the Germans remained immovable.

'The luncheon hour slipped by; four o'clock, five o'clock, passed. The delegates of several countries left, convinced that the Germans and Austrians had tried surreptitiously to evade acceptance of the only foundation of peace we knew.'

Thus the first contact with the ex-enemies was considerably soured. Further meetings over the next few years did little to dispel the impression that the German ex-service organizations were still controlled by diehards. There were such incidents as the handing back, by President Hindenburg, of the Gordon Highlanders' colours to Sir Ian Hamilton. The Legion itself kept up a tenuous contact with German ex-service movements, but there were no new major initiatives for a decade: till

November the eleventh, sir —thank you!

May I suggest, sir, that the money you have saved this year by smoking Kensitas—" *as good as really good cigarettes can be* "—at the price of ordinary cigarettes, be sent as a little thank-offering to Lord Haig's Appeal Fund—" *as good a cause as a really good cause can be.* "

Jenkyn

Kensitas
the preferred cigarette

'As good a cause as a really good cause can be.' Jenkyn, the butler in the Kensitas advertisement, helped to promote poppy sales in the 1920s.

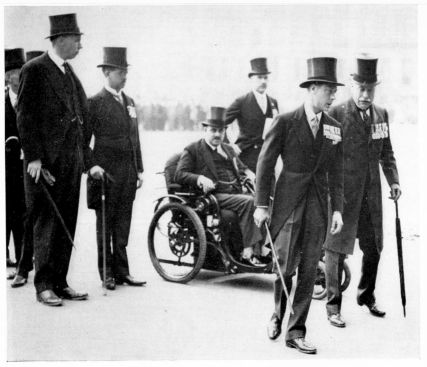

Legionaries with the Prince of Wales at the Palace. The tall figure
on the extreme left is T. F. Lister, the first Chairman.

'Without Haig there'd have been
no Legion. . . .' The first President
a few days before his death in 1928.
The wolf cubs were sons of disabled men at the Poppy Factory.

Pensions yesterday and today. Earl Jellicoe, in the centre of this deputation, succeeded Haig as President in 1928; on Jellicoe's right, Colonel Crosfield, second Chairman of the Legion; on his left, Sir Brunel Cohen.

A tribunal assesses a case in 1971. *Centre*: Sir Stafford Foster-Sutton, President of the Pensions Appeal Tribunals.

EAST INDIA DOCK GATES.

A MEETING

WILL BE HELD

On Sunday, April 15th, 1917

At 11.30 a.m. by

DISCHARGED SOLDIERS & SAILORS

To protest against being re-called to
the Colours again whilst Medically-fit
Men are being retained in Government
Workshops and Factories.

Chairman - G. NASH.
WILTSHIRE REGT.

SPEAKERS—

T. FITZGERALD   **J. PIPER**
(R.F.A.)   (MIDDLESEX REGT.)

Ex-Sergt. F. A. RUMSEY
(NORFOLK REGT.)

Ex-Sergt. Major MORRIS   J. BRANDON
(CANADIAN FORCES).   (ROYAL ENGINEERS).

AND OTHER EX-SERVICE MEN.

A further MEETING will be held in
VICTORIA PARK, at 3 p.m.

W. PETERKEN, Printer (Trade Union), 153 High Street, Poplar, E. 14.   Tel. 3358 East.

A handbill for a protest meeting
1917. Even before the Armistice
battle for ex-servicemen's rights
beginning.

By 1926 the Legion's great struggle was
against unemployment.

The First Seven Years will be the Worst!

Bruce Bairnsfather's original cartoon dated from the 1914 fraternization in the trenches. In 1935 the Legion *Journal* reprinted it to mark the exchange of visits between ex-servicemen from Britain and Germany.

The eleventh hour of the eleventh day of the eleventh month. . . . On Remembrance Day 1931, workmen on the scaffolding in Whitehall observe the Two Minutes Silence.

Preston Hall, the British Legion Village. The new Duchess of Kent Court will provide flats for sixty ex-servicemen and their families.

In the workshops disabled men work on Ministry of Transport road signs.

The war cemetery at El Alamein, where more than 7,000 British soldiers are buried.

By contrast the tiny cemetery at Mook, near Nijmegen, where 300 graves lie between lawns and flowerbeds.

after Hitler and the Nazi party had come to power in
Germany.

. . . .

On the whole the British are not good haters. It is
one of our more agreeable weaknesses if indeed it is one.
Now, however, this amiable national characteristic was
to lead the Legion to a situation of some embarrassment.
In 1937 an invitation to visit Nazi Germany reached the
Legion through the German Ambassador to London,
Ribbentrop.

That summer, at the Legion Conference, the Prince of
Wales had already given the idea of Anglo-German
friendship what seemed a unique accolade:

> 'There is one point which your President, when I
> was speaking with him the other day, brought up, and
> which also commended itself to me, and that was that
> a deputation or a visit might be paid by representative
> members of the Legion to Germany at some future
> time. I feel that there could be no more suitable body
> or organization of men to stretch forth the hand of
> friendship to the Germans than we ex-servicemen, who
> fought them and have now forgotten all about it and
> the Great War.'

The effect of the Prince's speech was immediate. It was
widely reported in the newspapers – and earned the
Prince himself a mild lecture from his father on the un-
wisdom of mixing in politics, especially foreign affairs.
Meanwhile from the German point of view, the effect of
the speech was highly desirable. Ribbentrop writing in
his memoirs of a period after the Prince of Wales'
accession, went out of his way to recall it:

'Edward VIII had shown his sympathy for Germany on several occasions. He had warmly supported a meeting of German and British leaders of ex-servicemen's organizations, which I had arranged. In his address at that meeting he had said that no one was better fitted to promote good Anglo-German relations than the men who had faced each other from the trenches. The speech attracted considerable attention, because as is well known an English monarch rarely makes a speech.'*

Whatever the meanings attached to them by German propaganda, by mid-July two Legion delegations were on their way to visit ex-enemy countries. The first of these was not to Germany itself but to Czechoslovakia and Austria. It consisted of Major Brunel Cohen and Colonel Ashwanden, the National Vice-Chairman. Brunel Cohen had originally been invited to Germany. As a Jew, he wrote later, his position had not been easy:

'Germany being the most important of the countries (to be visited) it would have been proper if I, as one of the three senior officers of the Legion, had joined my colleagues in a visit to that country. The idea of this, however, stuck in my gizzard and after much thought I decided that it was impossible for me to shake Hitler by the hand, and I decided, therefore, to visit the other three countries with the Vice-Chairman of the Legion, Colonel Ashwanden, instead. There was a great deal of correspondence in the Press, particularly in the Jewish papers, criticizing me for even having contemplated going to Germany, so much so that at a subsequent Legion conference I had to defend myself.'†

* *The Ribbentrop Memoirs* (Weidenfeld and Nicolson, 1954), p. 67.
† COHEN, Brunel: *Count Your Blessings* (William Heinemann, 1956), p. 106.

The second delegation was headed by Major Fetherston-Godley, the National Chairman. Leaving for Berlin on 13 July, they visited disabled men's settlements, met ex-service leaders, and laid wreaths on the graves of both British and German soldiers. On 15 July they were received by Hitler who talked to the Legion officials for nearly two hours.

Relations between British and German ex-servicemen were now firmly secured, and over the succeeding months there were to be increasing contacts. A German U-boat commander visited Legion branches giving lectures on his wartime experiences; parties of German ex-servicemen visited Buckingham Palace and were taken to tea at the House of Commons; mascots, cigarette cases, and other battlefield trophies were restored to their owners both in Britain and in Germany. The *Journal* summed up the general mood by reprinting the 1914 cartoon by Bruce Bairnsfather which showed 'old Bill' shaking hands with a German soldier. 'So long mate, see yer when we're not so busy fighting', ran the caption. The unconscious prophecy after the 1914 fraternization, added the *Journal*, was now fulfilled.

Were the Legion leaders misguided in these almost euphoric attempts to keep friendship going in the face of Nazi intentions which were almost daily becoming clearer? Perhaps some of the leaders had a view of Germany which was oversimplified. Yet it is hard to say that any effort for peace is misguided, especially one so firmly based on the common hatred of war between old soldiers. The Legion, in a rapidly darkening situation, were doing their best.

In September 1938 the last and most impressive of German delegations visited Britain. Headed by the Duke of Saxe-Coburg Gotha, 800 former servicemen arrived in

Britain by ship, which was moored in the Thames.
Welcoming telegrams had been exchanged, but by then
the Munich crisis had developed, and Neville Chamber-
lain was already on his way to visit Hitler. Originally,
recalled Sir Brunel Cohen,

'it had been arranged that their leaders should lay a
wreath at the Cenotaph and that then the whole party,
which numbered nearly a thousand, should march past.
In the highly inflammable state of public opinion in
this country at the moment this was considered to be
unwise. The leaders therefore, very early one morning
before the traffic in Whitehall had really started, laid
their wreath, and in the afternoon in the security of
the gardens of Chelsea Hospital all assembled and were
given tea and marched past General Sir Ian Hamilton.

'They were mostly oldish men who had served in the
First War, all dressed alike in navy-blue suits and a sort
of yachting cap. Every one of them seemed convinced
that there was very little likelihood – if indeed any – of
war between Germany and England. Nevertheless, I
am quite sure, and was so at the time, that they were
all staunch supporters of the Nazi regime, otherwise
they would not have been allowed to have been of the
party, and I took everything they said with a grain of
salt. At the end of their visit, they left quietly and there
was no incident of any sort. Still we were all glad to
say "good-bye" and not "*auf wiedersehn*" to them.'*

* COHEN, Brunel: *Count Your Blessings* (William Heinemann, 1956),
p. 116.

5
A Promise Honoured

IN 1914 Britain had been, in Disraeli's phrase, two nations. It was not one nation by 1939, but the margin between the two had been blurred considerably. This was not only in the sense Disraeli meant – a definition according to class or money. In a more inward, meaningful sense the Britain which went to war in 1939 was a united nation.

Essentially the difference between the soldiers of 1914 and those of 1939 was a difference of attitude. The later generation were more educated than all but a few of the earlier one. They were more informed about the causes of war, and from the beginning they had a deeper detestation of it – coming from a generation whose fathers had known the Somme and Ypres, they had few romantic illusions.

Also they had a healthier scepticism about politicians' promises. They were prepared to fight and die if necessary in a cause which in the deepest sense they understood to be a just one. They were not prepared to fight and be killed for nothing, nor were they prepared to come back to a Britain of unemployment, the dole, and the scrap heap.

In a sense the Legion had helped to create this new, more realistic attitude – but how was the Legion to cope with the new demands that were clearly going to be made upon it? How could it best help the new ex-servicemen, while still keeping faith with the old? Would the Legion's finances stand up to the strain of helping two generations of ex-servicemen? Would the proceeds of Poppy Day, for instance, go to help the wounded of two world wars or one? Would there in fact be a Poppy Day at all? In September 1939, there seemed no clear answers to these looming questions.

In the event the Legion need not have worried. Poppy Day was held in 1939 – and the proceeds went up to a record of £595,000. Unexpectedly, too, the amount of money needed to help the disabled and unemployed fell sharply. Wrote T. J. Birrell, of the benevolent department:

> 'The thing that surprised us was that ex-servicemen of the First War, sick, disabled, bent under the toll of years, got jobs in munition work and began to earn again. If they could walk they could work seemed to be their motto. It was a tribute to their fine spirit.'

Meanwhile the proceeds from Poppy Day continued to rise dramatically. In 1941 they reached £756,000; in 1942, £822,000; in 1945 the collection was well over £1,000,000 – almost double the 1938 figure.

Even so the Legion's greatest achievement was still to come. Through the 1920s and 1930s its headquarters staff had hammered away at successive governments on pensions, and also on the old question about the compulsory principle in the employment of the disabled. Now, in the greatly changed social climate of war, the Government was at last prepared to listen. In December 1943, the ruling was revised which had said that a claimant must prove that a deterioration in his condition was due to his service. From now on the onus of proof was to be on the State. The benefit of any doubt was to be in favour of the claimant.

At the end of the same year, 1943, the Disabled Persons (Employment) Bill received its Second Reading. Early in the new year it passed into law – the Legion had now reached the second of its great legislative milestones. From now on employers would be obliged to take on a quota of disabled men, and certain occupations would be officially noted as suitable for the disabled.

From 1939, the whole question of demobilization had engaged the Legion's attention. When the war ended, they were determined, there should be none of the chaos and unfairness which had characterized the 'key men' situation in 1919.

A Legion plan for demobilization was submitted to the Prime Minister as early as 1943 – when the Government's final plan was announced, its proposals ran almost parallel to those suggested by the Legion. (Indeed when Ernest Bevin sat next to Sir Gordon Larking at a Foreign Office dinner some years later, he confirmed this. 'You ought to thank me,' he told him, 'I adopted all the ideas and suggestions in your scheme.')

Thus the three major principles had all been won – pensions, the compulsion principle, demobilization. Thanks to the Legion, the returning serviceman in 1945 would come home to a very different Britain from that of 1918. Now, for the first time, he would get a square deal as well as honour, a job as well as the thanks of a grateful nation.

In the past he had had to fight for these things, but this time he would get them as a right. That, above all, was the measure of the British Legion's achievement.

PART TWO

Today and Tomorrow

6
The Village

TILL now we have looked at the past; now it is time to
look at the Legion in the present. Properly speaking such
a survey would take us right across England, for there is
hardly a town or village today which has not got a Legion
branch, a Service Committee which looks after the
interests of all who have served in the forces. We cannot
see all of these, but we shall look at examples which are
typical of most. As it is, our journey will take us to Kent
and Lancashire, to the pit villages of County Durham,
and over the Welsh Marches to the blue-flanked hills of
Brecon.

Since we cannot look at every village, we begin with
the one known to Legionaries as *The* Village – Preston
Hall, near Maidstone.

.   .   .   .   .

'I always had a liking for the trade,' says Chip
Chipperfield, 'ever since I was a schoolboy in Hackney.
I'd twisted my ankle at football and they got me on to
help printing things for the school mag. Later on when
the Headmaster asked me if I'd thought of any particular
career, I said I wouldn't mind going into printing. So
my parents put up £40 for me to be apprenticed. In those
days it seemed a lot of money.'

Today Chip Chipperfield is manager of the printshop
at Preston Hall. Looking round the shop from his office

45

window, it isn't difficult to see the fascination. The hum and treading movement of big machines, the drawer-fulls of tiny, silvery type, like herrings gleaming in the net of a trawler. To the layman, one of the few crafts that is still, in the medieval sense, a mystery. The difference here is that of the thirty people working in the printshop more than two-thirds are war-disabled.

Chip Chipperfield is one of the disabled himself. He came out of the war with tuberculosis in 1945, underwent several operations in Preston Hall hospital, and began working in the printshop six years later. Though you wouldn't think it to meet him, he is still classified as seriously disabled. 'What it amounts to,' he says, 'is that I need to have a rest at lunch time. I go home and put my feet up for an hour or so, then I'm ready for the afternoon's work again.' He lives with his wife in one of the bungalows on the Preston Hall estate, where he runs a Sick Benefit Club for the welfare of less well-placed people in the Village. 'The way I look at it,' he says, 'is this. If it hadn't been for the Legion, I most likely wouldn't have been here now. I try to pass it on a bit, by helping others.'

.   .   .   .

Standing in nearly sixty acres between Aylesford and Maidstone, the original Preston Hall is recorded in the Kentish history books. It was the home of the Colepepper family, and notably of Thomas Colepepper, the lover of Henry VIII's fifth wife, Katherine Howard. Despite these distinguished annals, nothing of the Elizabethan house remains – the present Preston Hall was built in the 1850s. It was used in the First World War as a convalescent home for soldiers, then sold in 1920 to an organization called

Industrial Settlements Incorporated which used it as a kind of model farm for the disabled. In 1925 the Legion took over both house and training scheme. From the start they began to plan it on a much more ambitious basis.

The Astor Committee set up by the Government in 1919 had made important recommendations on tuberculosis treatment. Faced with the problem of 55,000 men who had contracted the illness while serving, they had urged the need of some kind of village settlement where a patient could not only be treated medically, but also given some light work and living accommodation in healthy surroundings.

With these recommendations in mind, the Legion began to plan boldly. When they took over Preston Hall, it was a somewhat gloomy, monolithic, Victorian pile surrounded by farmland stretching towards the Medway. Soon the Victorian house was one of a whole series of buildings. The Legion built hospital blocks, a church, a restaurant, village shop, workshops, and more than 120 houses for ex-servicemen and their families, who were known as settlers. Preston Hall became the British Legion Village, complete with the County Council's road signs announcing the fact to motorists approaching from London and Maidstone on the A20.

A new phase began with the setting-up of the national health service in 1948. The hospital and nurses home were taken over by the Ministry of Health; the workshops, village houses, and grounds remained the property of the British Legion.

At the time there was discussion on whether the hospital should have also remained independent. With hindsight, the Legion's decision seems not only right but historic.

Preston Hall has survived as one of the most successful examples of co-operation between the State and private welfare. Not only with the Health Service – today the Legion gets, for the benefit of disabled men, a complex system of training grants. Any disabled workshop is bound to make losses; thanks to its close co-operation with both Government and Local Authorities, the Legion today runs Preston Hall more economically than any other sheltered industry in the country.

Today Preston Hall provides work for 132 men, eighty-four of them severely disabled. The other groups are made up of less badly disabled men and a few fit ones. These are necessary to do the heavy work, and to help the workshops meet their production deadlines.

Even so, Preston Hall's chairman, Charles Busby, would like to see the severely disabled proportion still higher. 'Taking on a disabled man is a risk,' he says. 'You can give a man a lot of training and then find he's just not capable of doing the job. All the same this kind of risk is what we're here for.' Busby is a local estate agent, as much at home in the workshops as on his auctioneer's rostrum. Going round the printshop, he explains the involved economics of running an industry which has got to keep its losses within reason, and at the same time employ people who most firms would regard as unemployable.

Recently the printshop installed two expensive letter-press machines – as Busby takes me round they are turning out covers for the *Journal* at the rate of forty a minute. 'The point about these machines is that they mean more work. Not for the actual operator, who needs to be a fit man, but for the more seriously disabled who work in the binding and despatch departments.' Busby would like to get a third machine installed, but they cost £8,500.

'Having got a seventy-five per cent grant for the first two from the Ministry,' he adds wryly, 'we'll probably have to pay for the next one ourselves.'

It is an example of the kind of needle-edge calculation which would drive an ordinary management crazy – especially when Preston Hall also needs money to replace workshops and living quarters. Physically, it seems to the outsider, Preston Hall needs to adapt. Many of the workshop buildings are shabby, their relation with the others unplanned because they have grown up piecemeal. Other buildings were built as T.B. wards and operating theatres; today they provide slightly gloomy recreation rooms and canteens for the older single men.

Now that tuberculosis is no longer a major threat, what are the main categories of disabled people wanting to come here? The man who sees all of them is Christopher Wearne, who came here as General Manager in 1967, after being an executive with Eliott-Automation. 'Nowadays the typical case would be a middle-aged ex-serviceman,' he says, 'probably suffering from a respiratory disease or a heart condition.' Besides this the effects of many second war injuries are only now coming to the surface. 'A lot of people who made light of their injuries twenty years ago,' adds Charles Busby, 'are just beginning to find them troublesome.'

If a man is accepted as a trainee (Preston Hall calls them rehabilitants) his course of work will be carefully planned by Christopher Wearne and the doctor. 'Most likely he'll have just come out of hospital and not be in any condition to start normal work. He'll probably live in one of the hostel blocks and work about four hours a day. After that he may leave and return to normal industry outside – or we might take him on as a full-time worker. In that case we should try to find a house in the village where his family would join him.'

Family life of this kind has always been the central idea of the Village. In the carpenter's shop I talk to Charlie Stockford, whose memory of the place goes back for fifty years. His eight children have all grown up here, served in the forces, and married. At seventy Charlie Stockford still has the sprightly toughness which seems to characterize the First World War veterans. Talking to him is like listening to echoes from a vanished world. Charlie joined up at fourteen, was fighting in France before his fifteenth birthday. 'Loos, Armentieres, Vimy Ridge, Ypres. Then we had two years in Italy,' he grins. 'From mud to sunshine.'

He came out of the war as a T.B. case: when he came to Preston Hall it was still being run as a farming settlement. 'It was all pig farms, game farms,' he says. 'I used to work as livestock manager. Then the Legion took over, and they've done what the place is meant for. If it hadn't been for them, we'd have been on the floor.'

When he retires Charlie hopes to come back and work a bit if he's needed. Otherwise he has his gardening and rabbit-breeding. He keeps between sixty and seventy rabbits, some of which he puts on exhibition every year at the Maidstone County Show.

Has he, I ask, won prizes for them? Charlie grins again. 'If you want to see some cups and trophies, you want to see the ones I've won at darts. Down at the Bush at Aylesford. Fifty years tonight since I first played for them. Probably,' he adds nostalgically, 'they'll give me a bit of a celebration.'

Printing and carpentry are two of the main departments – Preston Hall also makes road signs and fancy goods. Eric

White, who manages the fancy goods, came here three years ago. A flight controller in the R.A.F., he had to leave the service because of stomach ulcers. 'I was just beginning to like the job when they checked me out,' he says cheerfully. 'Now I'm beginning to like this one too.'

The world Eric White presides over consists of crackers and paper hats, magic soaps, clothes airers, brooms, brushes, and ottoman work boxes on legs. 'We had to put legs on them,' he explains, 'or else they'd attract purchase tax.' All the same the clothes airers are the mainstay of the workshop: each year Preston Hall sells 20,000 of them. Another recently successful line is a miniature plant-trough, small enough to plant out a dozen or so primroses. Originally the workshop had been making a much bigger one. 'We only made the small trough as a sample,' says White, 'because our traveller got fed up with carting round the full-size one. So we made him the small size to show the retailers and they all liked it – they said they weren't so keen on the big one but they'd have a few dozen of the sample. We've sold 1,000 in two months, and we've just had an order for 500 more.'

Preston Hall also makes most of the road signs for the Ministry of Transport – the kind of thing they put on motorways, saying no mopeds, no learners, no U-turns. I talk to Jack Luckhurst, a Second World War man who got typhoid fever in Palestine. He had a thrombosis as a result and had to give up working as a nurseryman. Today, an intelligent, rather artistic-looking man in his middle forties, he works in the silk-screen shop – putting designs on to a kind of silk pattern, which is then transferred to the metal road sign. Sometimes, he says, the job can get boring. 'I like it when we get a new sign to do, and we've got to fathom how to get the glaze on.'

As we go out he tackles Charles Busby about working on fabric: couldn't the Signs Department do something interesting with that? Charles Busby says he'd never thought about fabrics, but he'll make a note of it. I sense a difference in attitude from the World War One generation. Wouldn't Charlie Stockford's generation, I suggest to Charles Busby as we go out, have been more inclined simply to do the work they were given?

Busby agrees, and says that Preston Hall's own attitude has got to be more inventive. 'We've got to compete on the open market where we can – we've moved a long way from being a cottage industry. People are too far away from both the two wars nowadays for there to be any kind of sentimental link-up with our products.'

Another result of this distance is that Preston Hall is now beginning to take in a few people who have not been in the services themselves but are the dependents of ex-servicemen. Stephen Hayman works in the Signs Department, cutting out the letters. Aged twenty-seven, he came here because he was suffering from muscular dystrophy; he is now married with two children and lives outside the Village. 'When I started work it was a bit depressing because there weren't any other young chaps. Now there are a few more coming in, and it's much better.' The point is that the Village is uniquely fitted to take local cases of young people suffering from diseases which make them unable to work at ordinary jobs.

The Legion accepts this fact and welcomes it as a sign of Preston Hall's adaptability; Charles Busby himself is proud of its national reputation as a rehabilitation centre. Even so, the ex-service need has not begun to diminish. As far ahead as 1995, Busby points out, there will be

110,000 men still living who fought in the Second War, and still a few hundred from the first one.

From the signs shop he takes me to the Duchess of Kent Court. A £120,000 block of flats for old people, this is part of the nationwide scheme begun by the British Legion Housing Association. Nothing I have seen at Preston Hall so far has prepared me for this – twenty-four double flats, sixteen single, in a block which could be an expensive new housing development in a commuter district. The rate for double flats is £4·90, for a single one £4·40, both inclusive of rates. An additional £1 a week is charged for heating and lighting.

'At this rate we reckon they'll have quite a bit over,' says Busby. 'Most of the people here will be having their rents paid out of their supplementary benefits. The immediate point of the flats is that they're for our ageing population. When a man retires from the workshops, it means his house is a loss to us. We can't kick the family out – and we'd like to make their remaining years more comfortable. Giving them flats like these makes sense all round. It takes away the onus of looking after a larger house and garden.'

Designed in tawny-coloured, brownish brick, the flats are all edged with white railings and patios. They surround a central forecourt where there are raised terraces, low walls, seats under the chestnut trees. Each flat has a balcony of its own looking either to the front or back; on the reverse side is a communal patio. 'The aim's to bring everyone into the social centre of the forecourt,' says Busby. 'A sort of mixture of privacy and involvement.' On the same principle there are communal rooms where the old people can get together and watch television or sit and chat in the evening. If any of them become ill or in difficulty, there is a flat for a warden whose job is to be unobtrusive till needed.

On the way back from the Duchess of Kent Court, we look at the living quarters for the rehabilitants. Many of these, Busby tell me, are older men whose greatest problem is not so much disability as the sense of being unwanted. About half of them live in the chalets – a row of rather depressing-looking, cream-painted, wooden huts.

'Would you mind if we had a look inside?' Busby knocks on the door. The chalet's occupant is one of the rehabilitants who works in the hospital. In terms of the size of the room he can hardly be said to show us round, for it is only about eight feet square. There is a bed, washbasin, shaving things, photographs, and writing paper – the sum of a lonely man's possessions. When we have left I wonder if I am supposed to make some approving noises, but Busby sticks his pipe back in his teeth angrily.

'Now you can see why I'd like to push a bulldozer through the lot.'

'If you do that what happens to the rehabs?'

He points to the old walled garden, which occupies several acres of the ground which slopes from here towards the Medway. Around us, apart from a few acres of hogweed, are a few fine cedars and beech trees, an old urn dating from the palmy days of the Victorian mansion. 'I'd like to see the whole factory area shifted down here towards the walled garden. Eventually we hope to get the Poppy Warehouse brought down here from King's Cross – it's occupying valuable land up there and it'd make sense as part of a works unit. Where the chalets are, we'd set about putting up a completely new housing centre. I'd like to build flats for the older rehabs. In a completely new block – bedsitters which would really be home, with

communal sitting rooms and balconies. There'd be more
new housing all round, and a green area in the middle.
A green space – it'd be the village's heart and centre.'

Will Preston Hall enter a new phase, potentially as rich
in service as its earlier ones? Given the material means,
the vision and imagination are there on the part of the
men who run it.

Before I leave Charles Busby says one more thing that
seems worth recording. 'Men who've served together and
lived together and roughed together, there's something
between them. You can't put your finger on it but it's
there. It comes to the surface when it's needed.' The
words could be a description of Preston Hall – or for that
matter, the British Legion.

7
The Goodhearts of Nijmegen

PROPERLY speaking war graves are not looked after by the British Legion – they are the responsibility of the Commonwealth War Graves Commission, which is in turn a department of the Ministry of Defence. The Commission looks after the upkeep and condition of 1,127,322 graves in 140 countries: those of all British soldiers, sailors, and airmen who are buried in foreign battlefields.

Nevertheless, the Legion is very much concerned with war graves. It arranges frequent pilgrimages to the war cemeteries. If relatives want a wreath laid or a photograph taken, they get in touch with the Legion. If someone wants to visit a son's or husband's grave but cannot afford to, the Legion will pay for their visit. Though the essential part of its work is to help the living, the Legion has never ceased to be aware of the nation's debt to those who died for it. In a sense, they are its deepest inspiration.

This chapter is the story of the war graves in one small area – the battlefield of Nijmegen and Arnhem in Holland. In a short account this one area must stand for many, for all the British cemeteries that stretch from Normandy to Italy, from Egypt to Singapore.

It must stand too, for the Peter Vermeerens in all the lands, who honour these graves and cherish them.

.   .   .   .   .

The address I have been given in Nijmegen is 617 Hatertseweg. Peter Vermeeren, who lives there, is a good friend to the Legion: a man who has done a great deal to help the families of British soldiers since the war.

I find the Hatertseweg and No. 617. It is a large, comfortable-looking house in the prosperous suburb of Hatert. Next to the front door is a sign with a poppy on it and the name of the Nederlands Oorlogsgraven Comite – the Dutch War Graves Committee. Mrs Vermeeren comes to the door. Her husband is at home, she tells me, but in bed suffering from a bout of malaria. All the same, when he hears that I am writing something about war graves, he will certainly want to come downstairs and see me. Meanwhile, will I come in and have a cup of coffee?

Five minutes later a small, tanned man appears who, malaria or not, seems to generate an almost electric vitality. I put him down as a youngish fifty-five – later I discover he is in his early seventies. Within minutes, the table and floor of the Vermeeren household is spread with scrapbooks and pictures. Nijmegen during the battle in 1944, pictures of British and Canadian soldiers, many scenes in the war cemeteries. Later in the scrapbooks there are more pictures of British families, often being entertained by Dutch hosts. Soon Peter is telling me about the other links there have been since the war, for instance the cross of nails from Coventry Cathedral, given by a local British Legion branch to the thirteenth century church of St Peter in Nijmegen.

'For twenty-five years the links have been strong,' he says, 'and there is no sign of them fading.' He tells me about a family in the nearby village of Limburg who looked after an airman's grave when he was killed there.

Later he was re-buried in the Jonkerbos Cemetery, but the family still regularly send money to Peter, for him to lay a wreath on it.

Among the Vermeeren's most treasured souvenirs is an inscribed copy of the autobiography of General Sir Brian Horrocks, who commanded Thirty Corps during the Battle of Nijmegen. I glance at the flyleaf, and see that the inscription begins: 'To Peter Vermeeren, the father of the Goodheart Family which has given so much help over countless years to British families visiting war graves near Nijmegen . . .'

'What,' I ask, 'is the Goodheart Family?'

Peter, despite the malaria, is putting on his hat and coat. 'We'll go for a walk round,' he says. 'I'll tell you about the Goodheart family on the way.'

. . . . .

Going down the path Peter begins to talk about the Battle of Nijmegen. 'Here at Hatert we were on the border of the battlefield. The Germans had dug trenches in the woods just beyond here – the British were this side of them.

'Where the Jonkerbos Cemetery is now there was a tank repairing centre. We had thirty or forty soldiers billeted in the house, and we got to know them like our own children. We hadn't got much fuel and the only place in the house that was warm was the kitchen. So we used to sit in there with the boys, and they used to tell us about their homes and their parents. Then came the morning the battle started in Hatert. So many of the boys who had been with us were killed.' He pauses, and I notice a small badge he wears in his lapel – a white cross on a red ground, the whole enclosed in a heart-shape. 'Because I'd got to know them so well, I always wrote to their parents. In a way, I suppose that was the beginning of the links between us.'

As we come to the dual carriageway outside Peter's house it seems almost impossible to imagine a battle at Hatert. The Sunday afternoon trek of cars, people pouring in to the fine new football stadium I have passed on the way here. It seems another world from the one Peter describes a few moments later, as we branch off down a small track past a farmhouse. Here in front of us are woods, mostly oak trees. We clamber over a fence, then he stops in front of a biggish rectangle of earth which looks as if it's been turned lately.

'This was the patch of ground where the soldiers first buried their comrades. At first there were three or four graves, then thirty, then by the end of a week or so there were four hundred. There were burials going on while planes were still fighting in the air. Many of the soldiers were unknown – there were seventeen of them at one stage, and there was one lady who said she'd adopt them, she and her children. That family looked after the unknown graves for years. They put fresh flowers on them long after the War Graves Commission had taken over.'

Peter breaks off the story and fingers a small oak sapling growing by the verges of the earth rectangle. 'These were the same saplings we put round the graves – we couldn't get any flowers in the town and these were growing close by so we planted them. Later of course the bodies were moved, but this was where we put them first. I remember it was very difficult because the soil was so sandy. We wanted black earth to bury the soldiers. We wanted to do it, you understand, in a proper manner.

'So people used to bring the black earth at night from other places. We had no bicycles or if we did have bicycles they had no tyres. People came from far out in the countryside on these rotten bicycles, bringing boxes of black earth and little bottles of flowers if they could get them. And so we dug the graves better, doing it by the light of a petrol lamp.

'In these first burials there was nothing but the wooden crosses – the army made them for their comrades, out of bits of wood. Then in front they put small glass jars or cigarette tins. The Chaplain would go round and put a man's own possessions in the jar – any diary or letters, how he had died and any last words he had said, so that his comrades would know, when they came to write and tell his people.

'I suppose it was about three months after this – three months after the beginning of the battle – that we had a kind of service of dedication. We were lent an altar by the church across the road here, and we took it over to the farm on a handcart. Apart from tending the graves, that was really all we could do till the end of the war – and then of course the War Graves Commission took over. They reburied the soldiers in the Jonkerbos and the other cemeteries.'

Peter stands looking at the rectangle of earth for a moment, then we turn and stroll for a bit in the cool October sunlight. We admire the fine new children's hospital which has been built in the woods, its grounds including the original burial-place. Jonkerbos itself, he points out, lies slightly to the left of us, behind the woods, which in the sun seem almost varnished to the red and yellow tints of autumn.

'But for the people of Nijmegen, it was in one way only

the beginning of the story. You know that now in Holland we have a Poppy Day, just as you do?'

I have heard, I remember, something of the sort, but I ask Peter to tell me more about it. The people of Holland, he explains, decided after the war that anyone coming from Britain to visit the war graves should be their guests. All their travel expenses once they arrived at the Hook of Holland should be paid for: no relative visiting a soldier's grave in Holland should be out of pocket for any possible item. This includes hospitality in the homes of Dutch people, though Peter stresses that no Nijmegen family would dream of allowing this to come out of the funds from Poppy Day.

'We must have had hundreds of organized pilgrimages by now,' he says, 'many of them staying for a week, the Canadians sometimes for ten days. When the Legion in London tell me there's a party coming over, I make the arrangements, and sometimes it's very difficult. Not because of finding places for them all to go, but because of leaving out all the families who want to have them. Everyone in Nijmegen regards it as an honour – I know one woman who's got a whole table cloth covered with the signatures of her visitors. In one of the biggest factories, every worker for years gave five cents every week off their payroll to entertain the British. But it wasn't the money so much – it was the feeling. The feeling that the British soldiers had given their lives in liberating us. We wanted to do any small thing we could, to make it easier for their people.

'Usually when a pilgrimage comes out from England, they go to the graves on the first day. Then on the Sunday there's a church service at the cemetery. Later the relatives make many visits back to the grave, but in the

meantime we take them round to a few places of interest –
the tulip fields if it's the right season, the canals in Amster-
dam, and so on.'

We come out of the grounds of the children's hospital,
and turn out towards the main road where Peter's house
is. 'I suppose it was out of this that the name came up, the
Goodhearts of Nijmegen. Once when we were having a
meeting I said we were a mixed lot of people, but all that
mattered was to have a good heart. Later Sir Brian
Horrocks got to hear of the name. He always calls us the
Goodhearts of Nijmegen.'

He turns, showing me the little heart-shaped red badge
in his lapel. 'We felt it was the right symbol, the cross
in the heart shape. It means that the boys who
are buried here have found a place in our hearts. I
gave one to General Horrocks, because he had always
taken a great interest in what we did for the soldiers'
families.

'I always remember once he came over here – it was
the occasion when your late King's brother, the Duke of
Gloucester, came to Nijmegen. There was a great ceremonial parade and a church service, and General Horrocks
was there to meet His Royal Highness.

'It was the sort of occasion you'd expect him to wear
all his war medals and decorations and so on, but he
didn't. He just wore the little badge of the Goodhearts
of Nijmegen.'

·   ·   ·   ·   ·

Later we get in Peter's car and drive over to the other
side of the wood, to Jonkerbos. I have seen some of the
World War One cemeteries before, the great fields of
crosses in the plains of northern France, but this is

different. Here one has the sense that every individual matters, a private resting-place among comrades.

As we come to the gateway I ask Peter what the name Jonkerbos means.

'I suppose you would say the wood of the lords in English. *Bos* means wood. *Jonkers* are a kind of aristocrat.' We go through the gateway. The name, it occurs to me, does not seem inappropriate.

In front of the gate is a kind of brick building, a pavilion. Inside it, Peter says, is the bronze door which you can open and take out the book inscribed with the name, regiment, and family of every man buried here. Beside the pavilion is a small plaque. '1939–45', I read. 'The land on which this cemetery stands is the gift of the Dutch people for the perpetual resting-place of the soldiers, sailors and airmen who are buried here.'

Past the pavilion, the cemetery stretches out behind a great stone cairn with one simple inscription – 'Their Name Liveth for Evermore'. At the far end from here stands a huge cross: between cross and cairn, the graves spread out in a crescent, flanked on each side by the woods. Between them are wide walks – often the graves are in fives, like groups of comrades. Above all there is not what one perhaps fears about a war cemetery – there is no sense of crowding. Here on the quiet lawns of Jonkerbos there is space. There is the feeling that you can sit down on one of the seats under the trees, or pause in the walks between the graves. There is the hint, almost, of an English village green; a feeling of quietness and openness.

There are one thousand six hundred and three graves in Jonkerbos; seventy-six of them, unknown. Each is marked with a simple headstone bearing the name, some words chosen by the family, and the regiment. Their names, as you pass the graves, are like some muffled roll of drums: The Grenadiers, The Life Guards, The Black Watch, The Duke of Cornwall's Light Infantry, The R.A.F., The Wiltshires. When a grave is unknown it is marked simply 'A Soldier of the 1939–45 War. Known unto God.' Round many of the graves are small flower-beds planted with climbing roses. Towards the pavilion is a great bank of heather, a line of yews by the broad grass walk that takes your eye to the cross.

We walk slowly towards it, then turn back to look at the great crescent of graves. I remember something I have been told earlier about the pilgrimages, by the wife of a Legion member who has often been here with her husband. 'After the initial shock of seeing the grave of a son or husband,' she said, 'the tension can be almost unbearable. But then there's the church service next day which all the relatives come to. In some way that's difficult to describe, this breaks the tension. After it the atmosphere changes – the tension goes, people are ready to talk much more happily, exchange memories with their Dutch hosts and so on.

'After the service, somehow, it doesn't seem to be a tragic occasion.'

·　　·　　·　　·

'Between the crosses, row on row . . .' One would imagine, wrongly, that all war cemeteries are the same. Later Peter drives me to the little graveyard of Mook, where five hundred British servicemen lie in a fold of wooded hills, where beyond a great bank of laurels there is a glimpse of deer grazing. Mook cemetery is one of the smallest in Holland, and the smallness gives it a dignity of its own: there is the sense of a band of brothers.

Different again is the Canadian cemetery of Groesbeek, which lies high on a hill to the south of Nijmegen, a great sweep of open country around it. As you walk between the graves of Groesbeek you look across a blue mist of wooded hills to the German frontier and the Reichswald, where the trees are only just beginning to grow again after they had been blasted by the Allied advance in 1945. Here on the crown of a high hill are two thousand three hundred graves, their regiments the roll-call of Canadian honour. The Lake Superior Regiment, you read, The Royal Hamilton Light Infantry, The South Saskatchewan Regiment, The Toronto Scottish, Le Regiment de la Chaudière. Here too on the walls of two great pavilions by the gate, are the names of many others. 'The names,' reads the inscription, 'of the Soldiers of the British Commonwealth and Empire who fell in the advance from the River Seine through the Low Countries and into Germany but to whom the fortune of war denied a known and honoured grave.'

On the way back I ask Peter about the German war graves – seeing the frontier has prompted me to ask about them. Most German soldiers who fell here, he says, are buried in their own country. He tells me of one British war widow who saw a vast German cemetery where thirty-two thousand men are buried.

She had looked at the cemetery for a long time, then turned to Peter. 'Now,' she said, 'there is no more hatred in our hearts.'

.   .   .   .   .

There is one other name that is for ever England in this part of the Dutch countryside: fifteen kilometres from

Nijmegen, the town of Arnhem where British paratroops landed in August 1944. Arnhem itself is only a few miles from Zutphen, where in an earlier battle Sir Philip Sidney had coined the image of English chivalry. Now, four hundred years later, the men who inherited that tradition lie in the little cemetery of Oosterbeek.

Oosterbeek itself is just down the main road from Arnhem, near to the hills where the landings were made. Within a great surrounding bank of rhododendrons the cemetery is laid out in the form of a cross. Here, like Jonkerbos, there is space to stroll down the side spaces between the graves, places to sit under the trees. What makes Oosterbeek different, I notice, are the numbers of people. In all the other cemeteries there have been twos and threes, but here there seems to be a constant stream of them. In the car park there are two or three cars with G.B. plates, but most seem to be ordinary Dutch people out for the afternoon.

When I ask Peter about this he takes me over to the pavilion by the gateway. 'Come and have a look at the visitors' book.' He opens the casket where in each cemetery the visitors' book is kept, next to the one with the names of those who are buried. He opens the book, turning over some of the pages where Dutch people have added comments. 'Our liberators will never be forgotten,' I read, 'We will never forget.' 'Dank voor all,' runs another – 'Thank you all.'

'You see. We never will forget.' Peter hands the book to me, and I browse over some of the comments that have been made by British families. 'My dearest boys,' reads one. 'This may be our last visit,' says another, 'to our dear son's resting-place. Thanks to all our dear Dutch friends. Dad and Mum.'

No words could express war more totally, its waste and pain and pity. Yet this is not the whole of Oosterbeek. There is also the calm and serenity of the green lawns, the memory of high courage. As the years go by there will be a new and continuing purpose – to remind future generations not to let it happen again.

8
Taxi!

THE scene is the classroom of the British Legion's Taxi School – probably the most unusual classroom in London. The pupils are mostly in their thirties and forties – intelligent, lively-looking men who sit at desks with note-pads and biros. There are few decorations in the room, some maps, and intricate sketches of various one-way systems.

'I'd like you to take me from Wilton Crescent to Belgrave Hospital for Children.' Mr Lardent is in charge of the class, a small alert man who might be in his early sixties. His eyes travel over the class, then light on a man in a leather jacket who is tapping cigarette ash into a small tin on the desk. 'Hooker?'

The leather-jacketed man gets up, a shade uncertain-looking. 'That's the Hospital for Children in Southwark Bridge Road?'

'That's the Evelina. The Belgrave's the one facing the Oval Station.' Mr Lardent's bearing is precise, the manner of a man teaching something intricate. We could be at a class learning some tricky principle of higher mathematics.

'Oh yes. I'm with you now.' Hooker, still standing, begins to recite his list of street names carefully. Occasionally there is one I have heard of. Mostly, I am lost in the involved geography of South London.

'Right into Durham Street. Left Harleyford Road.

Forward Harleyford Street.' Hooker's voice intones slowly. It is not a lesson learnt by rota, he is seeing the streets as he recites them. 'Right Kennington Park Road, forward into Clapham Road. The hospital's on the corner of Clapham Road and Prima Road.'

'That's all right.' Mr Lardent's words of praise tend to be moderate. All the same I notice the class like him, and are also fascinated – it seems unbelievable that one man could know so much about London. 'Any points about that? Why's Prima Road important? Well, it's the junction of two big thoroughfares, isn't it, Kennington Park Road, and Clapham Road.' He glances up at Hooker, a look of mild criticism. 'One other thing, you went straight from Harleyford Road to Harleyford Street. You forgot to say Kennington Oval.'

'Oval?'

'You've got to say Kennington Oval. People think it's only a cricket ground but it's not, for the cab driver it's a street too. There's three Ovals in London, Kennington, Brixton, and Hackney. Lord Montgomery was born at Kennington Oval as a matter of fact, in the Vicarage there. Used to be the old Oxford and Cambridge Club.'

. . . . .

The British Legion has some unexpected activities, but the Taxi School is unique. I found it in the district we have been talking about – a classroom and a few offices over a taxi-garage in Kennington. It was begun by the Legion in 1927, with the gift of a training taxi from Lord Nuffield. Now officially regarded as an Approved Training Centre, it is still run and maintained by the Legion. Its Superintendent, George Stedman, is a former Scotland Yard Inspector who worked as an examiner in the Public

Carriage Office. Apart from a few independent ones, the trainees here get a Government Training Allowance: most are disabled, though not noticeably. 'The typical trainee nowadays,' says Mr Stedman, 'is an ex-serviceman who's suffering from some back injury like a slipped disc. The doctor tells him he had better pack up his job if it means a lot of heavy lifting or standing.' Since it began the School has trained around 4,000 men – about one in three, Mr Stedman reckons, of London taxi drivers.

What does the training of a taxi driver involve? Basically it isn't a matter of driving, but geography. ('When you say Loughborough Road,' Mr Lardent's voice drifts in from the classroom, 'wouldn't it pay you to go by Hinton Road, Milkwood Road, and Half Moon Lane? You've got two ways and you've got to know them both. That's what it means to be a cab driver.')

Such almost pedantic knowledge of London streets comes only partly as a result of studying maps and books. The course can take anything between a year and eighteen months; the real guts of the work, says Mr Stedman, comes from a trainee's going round the London streets himself, usually on a moped. During the course he will be expected to acquire a complete knowledge of all the streets in a six-mile radius of Charing Cross. Later he learns, in slightly less detail, the suburban area, roughly from Watford to Reigate and Staines to Dagenham.

When the candidate is finally tested at Scotland Yard, his knowledge of the six-mile radius will be tested from a small, rather antique-looking document called the Public Carriage Office List of Questions. 'It's always called the Blue Book, although it's pink nowadays,' says Mr Stedman reflectively. 'It used to be blue in the days of the horse-cab.' Basically the Blue Book contains 460 specimen runs, plus embassies, clubs, theatres, and sports grounds. A 'run' is the shortest route from one place to another. The other key-word at the Taxi School is 'calling-over' – the recitation of street names in a route.

Before he goes to the Yard for his final interview, each candidate will have been there at various intervals for testing. 'They attend the Public Carriage Office every twenty-eight days,' says Mr Stedman. 'Towards the end of the course it may become every fortnight. If they think a man's not really working, then they'll make it every fifty-six days. That's very discouraging for a man – it means they think he's got to go back and do a bit more roadwork. Quite often a chap'll come and see me in the first few weeks – he'll get depressed and I'll have to bolster him up a bit. But on the whole, there's very few who don't make it.'

Mr Stedman presides over this arduous training schedule with the good humoured relaxation of a benign uncle. 'On the whole I have to be,' he says, 'when the blokes get really involved in all this it changes them, they don't think of anything but the knowledge. They've got maps stuck round the walls of their rooms at home and they spend all the evening calling-over. They wake up in the middle of the night, they start thinking of a run and they can't go to sleep till they've got it. The other day one of the wives came in to see me. She said her husband was always out in the evening, she was certain he'd got another woman. He was always coming in so tired, she said, just when she'd like a little cuddle. Well of course he hadn't got another woman, he was round with some of the other trainees, practising his calling-over. If you've got a lot of kids in a small flat you can't concentrate properly.'

It still seems to be a tough way of acquiring a skill. What, I asked Mr Stedman, are a taxi driver's likely earnings?

'It's always a difficult question,' he said. 'You get some of the older men, they sit about in a cab shelter and they don't earn much. You'll get others who work seven days a week. If they'll work evenings, weekends, Bank Holidays, they'll earn. They say the Income Tax people work on £25 a week, but it can be a lot higher. If a man isn't afraid to work, he can go on and get others working for him. We had one man through this School, he's a local Legion secretary by the way, and he's got thirty-eight cabs.'

While we are talking there is a knock at the door: a young driver who has just passed out from the School has come in to say goodbye, to collect his papers and certificate. Mr Stedman disappears and comes back in a few minutes. 'You might like to talk to this young fellow,' he says, 'what you might call a typical product.'

I say I would like to very much and Mr Stedman returns with a dark, goodlooking young man in his early thirties. He tells me his name is Tony Brennan and he has been a National Serviceman with the Iniskillings. 'Part of the time in Northern Ireland and the rest in darkest Wiltshire,' he says with a grin; he didn't actually get shot in Northern Ireland though three of his mates did, one of them in the right hand so he had to salute with the left one. Tony Brennan himself pulled his back shifting some barrels – 'Technically speaking I'm a disability. My brother's a cab driver – he owns a couple of taxis, so I thought I'd go in with him. The money's good, but what really attracted me was the freedom. Last year my brother and I were on holiday with our families, and at the end of the fortnight he said he felt like staying on another week. You can do that if you're a cab driver. It means you have to work a bit harder later on to make it up, that's all.'

I ask Tony Brennan about the course. His experience bears out what Mr Stedman has told me. 'My wife was under a bigger strain than I was,' he says. 'You don't get a lot as a trainee and the work's completely demanding. I used to spend the whole day out on the moped till half past four, then in the evening I went round to another trainee's house. We started at seven, didn't finish till ten-thirty. If we did a run and we weren't happy, we cottoned it up. Put a piece of cotton or string on the map, linking the two places you want to begin and end with. Then we'd work out the run of roads that went nearest to the string. After about nine months,' he goes on, 'I'd begun to get the hang of it – I began to know London. The average Londoner knows the way to somewhere, but he doesn't know the street names.'

Had there been many moments when he had thought of giving it up? Tony Brennan lights a cigarette and considers. 'It can be a bit bleak going round Mile End Road at half-past eight at night, your bike playing up, and pouring rain. What keeps you going is the *camaraderie* – a bit like being in the army.' I ask if most of the trainees are much aware of the Legion influence. Rather to my surprise Tony Brennan becomes very positive. 'If it hadn't been for the Legion part, I have serious doubts whether I'd have finished. The chaps helping you along, the comradeship.' Mr Stedman breaks in to say did I know there was a special branch of the Legion for taxi drivers? He is Vice-President of the branch himself – they use the headquarters of the Marylebone branch in Grotto Passage,

Paddington. 'Grotto Passage,' he repeats, savouring it, 'there's a nice name for you.'

Presently the conversation drifts off. Tony Brennan starts telling Mr Stedman about his examination at the Cab Office. 'You've got to hand it to them, they're clever. This examiner said to me, right, Peckham Police Station. What's the name of the street next to it, funny name? Well, fortunately I knew it, Meeting House Lane. Only he wasn't asking it like a question – what he really wanted to know whether I'd actually been there, not just read it in the Blue Book.'

Mr Stedman grins and looks up. 'Who was that, Mr Wicks?'

'Mr Wicks, that's right. He's got a photographic memory.'

'He should have,' says Mr Stedman. 'I taught him.'

From the examination we move on to hearing about Tony Brennan's first day as a driver, which was yesterday. 'How did you get on,' asks Mr Stedman. 'Did you have butterboy's luck?'

I ask what butterboy's luck is, and Mr Stedman roars with laughter. 'Beginner's luck,' he says. 'When a man's just got his badge, he's a butterboy. He might go down looking for a fare in the City at eight o'clock in the evening, and up comes one from the manholes. That'd be butterboy's luck.'

This takes us down a whole network of beguiling side-tracks when I ask about other examples of taxi drivers' slang. A mush is an owner-driver, I learn, a journeyman one who works for a big firm. Pill Alley to the Gasworks would be a run from Harley Street to the House of Commons. A legal is a fare who doesn't give any tip, a roader is a long journey. Eventually we get back to the subject of Tony Brennan's first day out with his taxi.

'Being honest,' he says, 'I was really nervous. Fortunately the first fare was a French lady, she didn't know whether I was making any mistakes or not. The second one was Notting Hill to Archway. He was a violinist, this chap, going to the music shop there. I said do you usually go through Swiss Cottage? He said I haven't got a clue, I'll follow you boy. Later on I got a bit confused taking someone to Drury Lane,' says Tony to Mr Stedman. 'The trouble is there's no entry from Russell Street.'

'That's right.' Mr Stedman nods sympathetically. 'And the theatre's not even in Drury Lane. It's in Katherine Street. Still, it sounds as if you didn't do too badly.'

Tony Brennan gets up to leave and we both wish him luck. 'That boy'll make a success of it,' says Mr Stedman with confidence, after he's gone. 'He'll make a cab driver.'

The Legion Taxi School, it seems to me, not only trains people – it teaches them the pleasure of doing a job properly.

9
The Story of the Poppy

'THE nation remembers one day in November. The Legion remembers all the year round.' Fifty years after its foundation, the Legion's essential inspiration is still the sacrifice of two generations of war-dead.

Over the years Remembrance has usually provoked controversy. Seldom a November goes by without some newspaper columnist declaring that the ceremony has become meaningless and outworn. In 1969, as a result of a motion put before the Church Assembly, the form of the Remembrance Service was revised, with a new accent on peace and rededication. It was prepared by a committee of churchmen on which the Legion was represented, and basically the new form was approved by it. (Though not without the protest of certain Legion diehards who opposed the introduction of a part of the service relating to penitence. Having spent four years in the mud and blood of Flanders, they said, not unreasonably, they did not entirely see what they had to be penitent about.)

How much is there in the claim that the Legion's remembrance is nevertheless too nostalgic, the sentimentality of old soldiers jingling their medals? Nowadays such claims are heard less often – even so, says Dennis Cadman, the Legion Chairman, it is still important for the feelings of ex-servicemen to be explained to young people. 'They've grown up knowing nothing of war,' he points out, 'and I think they've got the idea that Remembrance is somehow to glorify it. They see us at a village war memorial or the Cenotaph and they say "Don't they love it" – meaning wearing our medals, and so on.'

'What we still need to get them to see is how untrue this is. Ex-servicemen don't glorify war – they know too much about it. If you're an ex-serviceman and you go to the Cenotaph, you're not looking at an empty monument with an empty mind. You're remembering those you served with who didn't return. If someone's protecting your back one moment, and next moment you're burying him, you don't forget.'

.   .   .   .   .

For most people the British Legion means Poppy Day. Wear Your Poppy With Pride – it is the link between Legion and public. But why the particular stress on Poppy Day – and why, in any case, the poppy?

The origin of it all was a poem, written by Colonel John McRae, who in peacetime was a professor at McGill University, and who had landed in France with the first Canadian contingents.

During the second battle of Ypres in 1915, Colonel McRae had been in charge of a first aid post. At some point in the battle he found time to write a poem in pencil on a page torn from his dispatch book. Perhaps 'found time' is scarcely the right phrase – McRae was a professor of medicine, not a professional writer. And the words of his poem suggest that they must have come to him immediately, that they had risen unbidden from the depths.

'In Flanders' fields the poppies blow
     Between the crosses, row on row,

That mark our place, and in the sky
The larks, still bravely singing, fly
Scarce heard amid the guns below.

We are the Dead. Short days ago
We lived, felt dawn, saw sunset's glow,
Loved and were loved, and now we lie
In Flanders' fields.

Take up our quarrel with the foe;
To you, from failing hands, we throw
The torch; be yours to hold it high.
If ye break faith with us who die
We shall not sleep, though poppies grow
In Flanders' fields'.

After the battle Colonel McRae had sent the poem to *Punch*, anonymously and with no title. *Punch* had printed it, in their rarely used heavy type, under the title 'In Flanders' Fields.'

Three years after that Colonel McRae was gravely wounded. He was taken to a military hospital on the French coast. The third evening, just before he died, he asked to be wheeled on to the balcony from which he could see the Dover cliffs. Looking at them, he murmured the last line of the poem to his doctor.

'If ye break faith with us who die
We shall not sleep, . . .'

McRae was buried in the Canadian War Cemetery in the green folds of the downs above Wimereux, a few miles east of Boulogne, where on each Remembrance Day, a branch of the Legion still lays a wreath of poppies on his grave.

The Story of the Poppy

As a piece of literature McRae's poem was an end in
itself, one of the most memorable ever composed by a
soldier on the field of battle. But now as time went on it
also came to mean something more – the germ of an idea
which was to be handed on, first to one, then to another,
in the story of the British Legion Poppy. Among those
who read the poem in *Punch* was an American woman,
Miss Moina Michael, who at that time was working for
the Y.M.C.A. in New York. She was deeply moved with
it, so much so that she wrote some verses of her own in
reply to it. The result was perhaps not on the same level
as McRae's grave music – all the same as a link in the story
of Poppy Day it is worth quoting.

> 'Oh! you who sleep in Flanders' fields,
> Sleep sweet – to rise anew;
> We caught the torch you threw,
> And holding high we kept
> The faith with those who died.
>
> We cherish, too, the poppy red
> That grows on fields where valour led.
> It seems to signal to the skies
> That blood of heroes never dies,
> But lends a lustre to the red
> Of the flower that blooms above the dead
> In Flanders' fields.
>
> And now the torch and poppy red
> Wear in honour of our dead.
> Fear not that ye have died for naught;
> We've learned the lesson that ye taught
> In Flanders' fields.'

Moina Michael obeyed her own precepts. From the
time she had first read *In Flanders' Fields*, she had decided

always to wear a poppy. Part of her work for the Y.M.C.A. in New York was running a hostel for secretaries working with foreign military delegations, and on 9 November 1918, a group of them decided to make a collection in appreciation of her kindness. When the presentation was made she told the secretaries that she intended to use the money to buy twenty-five red poppies, at the same time showing them McRae's poem and her own answer.

From New York the story moves to London, where three years later a French woman named Madame Guerin arrived at British Legion headquarters. Madame Guerin, it seemed, was connected with an organization which manufactured poppies and sold them for the benefit of French ex-soldiers. Would the Legion, she enquired, be interested in buying poppies as a means of raising money?

Mme Guerin remains a shadowy figure in the Legion's annals. There is perhaps a hint of commercial-mindedness in her original approach, but there was also something else. She had been one of the group of wartime secretaries who had known Moina Michael in New York, and had subscribed to the gift of the twenty-five poppies. Her interest may have been partly commercial, but in this way at least the link went back direct to McRae.

To the Legion officials, meanwhile, the idea of the poppy as a symbol of remembrance was a completely new one. Most of them knew McRae's poem. All of them knew the Flanders poppy, the frail-petalled flower that had so often dotted the battlefields scarlet. They seem to have hesitated briefly, then decided in favour. In the *Journal* that August, the suggestion was made that people should wear a small red poppy in token of Remembrance.

The first Poppy Day was held on 11 November 1921. It raised £106,000, but it also did something more. From now on the British Legion would become something more than an organization. With the coming of Poppy Day, it would strike deep into the hearts of the British people.

．　．　．　．

Meanwhile for the Legion itself, the coming of Poppy Day had suggested a new idea for enterprise. If poppies were to be sold, why should they not be made by British, rather than French disabled ex-soldiers? In 1922 the Poppy Factory, founded by Major George Howson, began work in a small room over a shop in Bermondsey. At first the workshop only made simple poppies – the suggestion of larger ones for wreaths came from the Prince of Wales, who on Armistice Day 1924 laid the first wreath made by the Poppy Factory on the Cenotaph.

By 1926 the number of men employed had risen to fifty. It became necessary to look for larger premises, and the factory moved to Petersham Road, at the foot of Richmond Hill. Six years later the numbers had expanded still more – new premises were built, including sixty houses and flats for employees and their families. Today the factory is still at Petersham Road, though the current rebuilding scheme will greatly improve its facilities. This includes the new £34,000 office block, canteen and reception area, and twenty-two new flats being erected by the British Legion Housing Association.

Thirty million poppies will be sold on the streets this November. All of them will have been assembled or in some way handled by ex-servicemen. Thus the link goes back direct to Flanders Fields – by way of the Poppy Factory.

．　．　．　．

'There'll be a need for all this as long as there's a single disabled man left in Roehampton or Richmond.' I forget who had spoken these words – someone, I think, at Legion Headquarters. They come back to me as I climb the Poppy Factory's office, past the flags and the portrait of Haig, the wheelchairs left by the entrance. The replica of the Queen's wreath in the front hall; ashes from the Field of Remembrance to be scattered over graves in British war cemeteries. It is all, you feel as you enter, part of the Legion legend.

But there is another side to the Poppy Factory: 164 men work here, all ex-service, most of them badly disabled. Beyond this the Factory provides work for another eighty housebound ex-servicemen. The full-time employees range from old soldiers like Alfred Fribbins, who goes back to Major Howson's time in Bermondsey, to Noel Davies, a coloured Nigerian who came here after an accident while he was serving in the R.A.F. in the 1950s.

As in any disabled workshop, there are really two aims: to produce poppies efficiently, and to give employment to men who would not easily find it elsewhere. The two aims often seem irreconcilable, but they work. 'Our job,' says Denys Simpson, the General Manager, 'is to achieve a balance. Overall we're firmly limited to the amount that Legion headquarters is prepared to spend on poppies. Within that, we're able to employ a lot of people whose output is minimal.'

If you're running a disabled factory, says Mr Simpson, even the weather can be a hazard. 'One year when we were snowed up, the factory lost 24,000 man-hours in three months. You can't expect a chap with one leg to come to work in the ice, and the cold's bad for respiratory cases. One way and another our Sick Benefit Club takes a caning in the winter. Then you get some chest cases that are worse in warm, dry weather. From this point of view, you can't win, really.'

Despite this, the Factory has never yet failed to meet its deadlines. Last year thirty million poppies were delivered to the Legion Warehouse, twenty thousand special poppies for altars, another five million poppies for wreaths on war memorials. Besides this there is a special department producing 100,000 rosettes and badges, mostly for special orders – a badge for Chelsea Directors for the Cup Final, a rosette for the Twickenham and District Best Budgerigar.

How does the Factory achieve this rate of production with a staff problem that most employers would give up as hopeless? 'Basically it's a question of fitting the job to the man,' says Bill Mutimer, the Personnel Officer. 'For instance there are plenty of jobs a one-armed man can do as well as if he had two arms.'

It is a problem Bill Mutimer knows about – he lost his right arm in 1941 when his ship was sunk by the *Scharnhorst*. Today he is a local J.P. and has just taken his Advanced Motorists Test; before he came here, he worked as a project engineer in industry. 'They bet me I couldn't do the job, because you needed two hands for a slide rule, stopwatch, pen, and clipboard. I went away and designed a special clipboard and they had to admit I could do it.'

Because of his own disability he has been able to help a lot of people in the factory – 'they think if he can do it, I can'. On the way round the factory he points out examples of fitting the job to the man. A one-armed man is at work on the veining machine which takes the flat shapes of the poppies and crimps them into cup-shapes. After a few moments, it becomes strainful merely to watch

the speed and deftness with which the operator drops
sixty-five poppies on to a revolving disc each minute.
'Let's face it,' says Mutimer as we move on, 'a two-
armed man couldn't do it quicker.'

Often a man will come here when he has been rejected
by many other employers – if so, it is Bill Mutimer who
has to decide if they can take him. 'You might get a chap
coming along with a bad chest. If so, I have to tell him I
don't think he can work with wreaths, because of the hay
in them. Then he'll come clean and tell me he's got a
cardiac condition as well – it's because of this he's been
turned down by everybody. I tell him it's just because of
this we *are* going to employ him. Helping the people who
no one else will, is what we're here for.' Not long ago the
Factory took on a man who'd been unable to get work
anywhere else. He was here three years, then died after a
heart attack. Afterwards his widow wrote saying the
three years had been the happiest of his life – he'd felt he
was no longer on the scrap-heap.

Even so security and employment is only part of the
point. The other thing the Factory provides is comradeship. 'You come back here and it's blokes,' says Sidney
Smith in the despatch department, an old Eighth Army
man. 'You come back to the army style, it gets you.'
'Because everyone has a disability, nobody minds talking
about theirs,' says Sid Shipman who got blown up by a
mortar bomb on D-day. If the use of his legs goes a bit
stiff from sitting, nobody minds if he gets up from the
bench and has a stroll to stretch them. Paralysed from the
waist down, Peter Brooker gets about on calipers and is
the supervisor of Rosettes and Badges. 'If my car breaks
down there's always someone to take me home,' he says.
'If the other chap's breaks down then I take him.' The

atmosphere is reassuring, almost jaunty – pin-ups on the wall and wheelchairs, a warm beating heart of Service sentiment.

In the Rosettes workshop I talk to Fred Groeger, who goes back to the old Bermondsey days with Major Howson. He tells me how he used to paint the poppies red enamel and black in the centre, how the disabled men's wives used to push them to work in wheelchairs. It seems a far cry from today, the squads of disabled men's cars drawn up in the car park. Fred Groeger has done forty-eight years in the Factory – he'll retire, he says, when he's done fifty. 'Speaking unofficially,' says Mr Simpson, 'we've got one or two that ought to be retired. The point is they love it and they wouldn't keep going if they couldn't come here.'

How does a disabled factory work out its rates of pay? 'Properly speaking,' says Bill Mutimer, 'we ought to have a special rate of pay for everyone.' In the General Manager's office we study an involved-looking schedule which lays down minimum wage rates. It is issued by something called the Ostrich and Fancy Feather and Artificial Flowers Wages Council. 'They couldn't fit us in anywhere else,' says Mr Simpson with a grin, 'that's how we got caught up in that lot.' From the schedule he explains the basic point which is that a disabled man gets the same money for a slightly slower rate of production – though in fact the Legion will always pay a couple of pounds or so over the minimum.

'A two-armed man working at full efficiency turns out 17,600 poppies in a week – he earns £16·73. Full efficiency for a one-armed man means less poppies – he gets the same money for turning out 13,200. You get a man in a wheelchair – he takes longer to go to the toilet, or to get a new box of supplies when he's finished one. So he gets his £16.73 for 16,200 poppies.'

Before I leave Mr Mutimer takes me over to the department where they are making the wreath for the Queen to lay on the Cenotaph in November. It has begun to be assembled on a huge white frame padded with straw—the poppies are special silk, waxed ones. Someone else is at work on a map of Australia in poppies; there is a floating one for Air Sea Rescue, which will be set adrift in the Channel on Remembrance Sunday.

.   .   .   .

The story of the Poppy Appeal does not end at Richmond. From there the box-loads are sent to a huge warehouse next to King's Cross station.* Captain Reginald Tickner, the man in charge, not only presides over thirty million poppies. He is also directly responsible for organizing the appeal, and for getting back a sum of around one and a quarter million pounds annually. Much of the local organizing is done by the Legion Women's Section. Captain Tickner is in touch with 5,500 groups in Britain, not to mention 232 overseas, from Moscow to the Falkland Islands. ('They've only got a population of about fifty, but they sent back £380 last year.')

Because the Legion's aims are nowadays getting across to a broader public, Captain Tickner believes, the proceeds from Poppy Day are rising. 'Over the last four years there's been a steady climb in the total,' he says. 'With the exception of 1969, which was a bad year for weather.' He

---

* Though not, probably, for much longer. By the summer of 1971, according to present plans, the warehouse will have moved to Preston Hall. This will mean not only a new modern building for the warehouse, but a handsome capital gain for the Legion.

attributes the increase mostly to better public relations, and especially the slogan 'Wear Your Poppy With Pride'. Five years ago the Legion was at a low ebb, from the point of view of getting publicity. It had a Mass Observation survey done in 1967 – barely one person in three knew anything about its work. Since then the Legion has taken its public relations much more seriously, and press and television coverage has improved accordingly. 'Miniskirted collectors on Poppy Day,' says Captain Tickner, 'may not go down too well with some of the older members, but they're certainly helping to bring in the money.'

Even so Captain Tickner stresses the need for still more collectors. Over the last ten years, 50,000 of the older generation of collectors have had to give up; one of the most urgent needs is to get more help from among the teenage generation. Because of this Captain Tickner goes round explaining the Legion's aims to young people in youth clubs, schools, and colleges. 'Young people today want to know the hows and the whys and whens. They want to discuss things and argue. But once you really get talking to them,' he says, 'you couldn't have a finer band of collectors. I tell them about some of the thousands of old boys who are really in need – and gently make the point that if it hadn't been for what they'd done in the past, we wouldn't have this freedom to argue.'

Clearly the approach to youth is paying off: Captain Tickner quotes an example when he talked recently to Social Science students at Bournemouth Technical College. 'Without any prompting, the local organizer got forty volunteers from the College,' he adds. 'That year the Bournemouth collection went up by £1,000.'

·   ·   ·

In recent years the suggestion has sometimes been made that the whole organization of Poppy Day could be made simpler. The poppies themselves could be made of paper and pins and assembled by teenage girls in Basildon, who would not really know what they were making. This would greatly reduce the cost, and it would probably also reduce the takings – the one and a quarter million pounds which Poppy Day yields each year, and which is the Legion's source of income.

Such a change would not only put 250 ex-servicemen out of a job – it would also take away something of the emotion which is the Legion's centre. There is something about Poppy Day which sets it apart from all other flag days. And the something is inextricably linked to the Poppy Factory.

10
The Further Shores

WHAT happens if a Canadian family want to visit their son's war grave in Holland? Or if a Jamaican ex-service-man falls on hard times? In one way such things are not the Legion's direct responsibility. In another sense they are part of the wider sense of comradeship which Haig had always envisaged.

Haig's absence from the Queen's Hall Conference of 1921 was not because he felt that, having secured unity, he could now leave the work to others. Early in 1921, he had set out for South Africa. The situation there was much the same as it had earlier been in Britain – four separate organizations each claimed the right to speak for ex-servicemen in South Africa. In February 1921 a conference was convened at Cape Town and opened by General Smuts. Its purpose was not only to achieve unity in South Africa itself, but also to set up a wider organization, which would look after ex-servicemen's interests throughout the Empire. This would be the first step, said Haig:

'in the formation of an Empire Legion which shall link all ex-servicemen together, which shall preserve among us the spirit of comradeship we formed in the Great War and guarantee for all time throughout all parts of our wide Empire the maintenance of the high ideals for which we fought. That is the object upon which I have set my heart now the war is over . . .'

The resolution calling for an Empire Ex-services League was proposed by the blind V.C. Captain Towse, and seconded by an Australian, Comrade Dyett. (Throughout the proceedings, it seems, all delegates were referred to as 'Comrades'.) Thus the formation of the British Empire Services League was the beginning.

Four years later Haig toured Canada, where he found as many as fourteen ex-services organizations. He persuaded the leaders of all the groups to unite together. The Unity Conference in Ottawa in 1925, was the beginning of what is now the Royal Canadian Legion.

Haig had planned to visit Australia and New Zealand as well, but he never lived to do so. On the 29 January 1928 he died quietly at his brother's house in London, the last act of his life being to write a letter on Legion business.

.   .   .   .   .

In 1971 the links forged fifty years earlier are strengthened, even enlarged, from Haig's original concepts. Today the Empire Services League has been re-named the British Commonwealth Ex-Services League, and serves the needs of ex-servicemen in more than thirty-six countries. In Australia, 300,000 members of the Returned Services League are evidence of a comradeship and dedication to service comparable to the British Legion itself. Australia has a full Government ministry devoted to the interests of ex-servicemen, known as the Ministry of Repatriation. *Reveille*, the journal of the New South Wales branch, is read by 124,000 ex-servicemen in one state alone: youth groups, motel clubs, and women's auxiliaries branches are clear signs of the movement's confident approach to the future. Despite South Africa's having left the Commonwealth, the South African Legion continues to be affiliated to the League, including the members of the Coloured Ex-Servicemen's Legion. In fact South Africa is not the only non-Commonwealth country in the League – Eire is also a member and so is the tiny Himalayan country of Nepal. Because the Gurkhas who live there have one of the proudest names in military history, a special arrangement has been made to include the Gurkha Ex-Servicemen's Association.

Canada has a national membership of over 250,000, and a Department of Veterans' Affairs within the Government. Among other work for ex-servicemen the Department directly supervises 'Vetcraft', the poppy-making workshops which work in close contact with the Royal Canadian Legion.

By 1985, the Department of Veterans' Affairs recently calculated, there will be more than half a million World War Two men over the age of sixty in Canada. To meet the growing need of help for the infirm among them, the Minister for Veterans' Affairs recently opened the new fourteen million dollar St Anne's Hospital in Quebec, which has 678 beds for permanently disabled men, as well as some of the most advanced research and treatment departments in Canada.

. . . . .

Thus in Australia, New Zealand, and Canada the record of service stands, if possible, even higher than in the past. What about the newer countries of the Commonwealth? In the First War, mainly Britain itself and the old dominions had been actively involved. One thinks of such names as Gallipoli, Delville Wood, Vimy Ridge – and then automatically of the Anzacs, the South Africans, and the

Canadians. But in the Second War a far wider range of Commonwealth countries were involved. Malaya, Burma, Hong Kong, and Singapore were overrun; major battles were fought in India and East Africa. In the first war West Africa raised thirty thousand men, none of whom went overseas. In the second war ten times that number were recruited, including two famous West African divisions which fought in Burma.

Thus after the second war the Commonwealth need was not only greater but more complex. The problem the League faced has been recalled by its Grand President, Earl Mountbatten of Burma:

'it was plain that the League needed to do something very much more positive . . . its validity and vigour was in danger of being called into question; it was also open to accusations of bias and discrimination in that the bulk of the help hitherto afforded by the League had been to those of British stock. In fact one-third of all Commonwealth ex-servicemen are outside this category.

'What was needed was for the League to prove by its actions that it was keeping abreast of events; that it no longer existed to serve only the faithful seven countries which had been represented at Cape Town in 1921, for by 1960 the family had grown to comprise forty-two different ex-service organizations in thirty-six Commonwealth countries.'

Given such a vast geographical area to work in, what could the League really do to help? Clearly the greatest problem was how to contact ex-servicemen, often in outlying territories, who were suffering hardship because of old age, sickness, or poverty. Before this could be done, though, a more sophisticated system of communications was needed. Operating as it does from a small office over an art shop in Bond Street, how could the League provide an adequate communications centre for areas as outflung as Nepal and Singapore, the Windward Islands, and Malawi? In the early 1960s Brian Roberts, the high-ranking ex-airman who is the League's Secretary-General, set off on a series of fact-finding tours of 78,000 miles through thirty-six Commonwealth countries.

The needs he found were even greater than had been imagined; often there were no practical channels for dealing with them. But as a result of his tours much closer contacts with local branches were set up. A welfare fund was begun with an initial subsidy of £11,000. (Most of this came from the bigger organizations in the United Kingdom, Canada, and Australia, but even the tiniest ex-service groups in the Caribbean made some contribution.) Because resources were still small, the help produced was at first in the form of pilot schemes. On the other hand the League was now in a position to put its finger on where the needs were most urgent – a land settlement scheme for ex-servicemen in Uganda, a gift of fifty sewing machines so that disabled ex-servicemen in Pakistan could earn a modest living as tailors. In British Honduras, Brian Roberts came across an elderly ex-serviceman who had lost his house in a hurricane. 'Everything he had was flat,' says Roberts, indicating his own desk in the office in Bond Street. 'Nothing higher than the top of this desk. We got him a grant of £70 from the local branch, and a bit from one of two other local charities. Today he's got a house to live in, but before we came along, all he got was sympathy.'

Apart from welfare, Roberts stresses the importance of

the League as a contact agency. If a Pakistani ex-service-man comes to Britain and needs help, then the League will put him in touch with the local branch of the British Legion. If a British ex-serviceman emigrates to Canada and gets in difficulties, then the system works in reverse. 'You may get a chap who does well till he gets to Canada,' says Roberts, 'then things may start to go wrong. Suppose he gets ill, he's got a wife and family to keep, and there's no National Health Service. We put him in touch with the Royal Canadian Legion and they'll look after him.'

What about race relations within the organizations of thirty-six countries? Brian Roberts seems surprised I have thought the question relevant. 'Bad race relations don't exist as far as we're concerned. If you take the ex-service community – seventeen million of us – we're all one brotherhood. A man's race and country of origin are of interest – but no more.'

Today the Commonwealth Ex-services League's annual expenditure is around £50,000. Essentially Brian Roberts sees this as coming from the stronger membership organizations to help the weaker ones. 'Today the richer countries are helping not only with general financial aid, but also in terms of taking on an individual commitment,' he says. 'Recently the President of the Royal Canadian Legion toured the Caribbean on a specific scheme for Canadian help, while the Australians have particularly looked after south-east Asia.'*

As a result of Australian initiative, the ex-service association of Malaysia is currently developing an impressive plan for building on a central site in Kuala Lumpur. This will include a new National Headquarters, and the rest of the accommodation will be let off to

* For the British Legion's own contribution, see p. 137.

commercial enterprise. The result will be a substantial guaranteed income for Malaysian ex-service welfare work. The scheme has already been backed by the League with a grant of £5,000: the Returned Services League of Australia, the sponsoring body, has put up 10,000 Australian dollars: the New Zealand Returned Services Association has put up a further 3,400 N.Z. dollars. The Malaysian Government has agreed to treble the total, making a final yield of around £100,000 – a formidable investment in Malaysian ex-services welfare.

Sometimes a member country finds itself in a special position to help another, as recently when the Ghana Legion ran into difficulties over its fund-raising lottery. Because the lottery tickets were printed in Britain and Ghana had little overseas currency to spare, they had difficulty in paying for them till the League made a special arrangement to help them. 'That's what I'd call a really practical way of spending our cash,' says Roberts. 'A comparatively small outlay from central funds meant the Ghana Legion were able to raise a much greater sum by their own efforts.'

More ambitiously, the League has also recently helped with the capital costs of new projects. One recent example is the Corps of Commissionaires, sponsored by N.E.W.A., the Nigerian Ex-Servicemen's Welfare Association. Not unlike the Legion's own Attendants Company, the Nigerian Corps is meeting a real need in a country where unemployment is a serious problem. The League gave them a start with £2,000 to buy uniforms – today the N.E.W.A. is employing 300 men and making an annual profit of £1,500.

Above all, Brian Roberts sees such links as strengthening the Commonwealth at its deeper levels: through the ex-service bond, help and ideas can be exchanged in a wider, more generous spirit of comradeship. For many of the new countries, aid from the older ones can point the way for better welfare services. 'Rather as the British Legion helped to pave the way for social justice in the past in this country,' he says, 'we can help them to achieve a better life in the future for all their people.'

11
Morning in Store Street

Store Street, W.C.1. – it is one of the West End's less notable side streets. Running between Tottenham Court Road and Gower Street; it links the world of department stores with the book shops and bicycles of Bloomsbury. Staffordshire House, the rather grandiose Victorian block on the right, is the London headquarters of the Pensions Appeal Tribunal.

I have come to Staffordshire House to hear a pensions case; on the second floor I am to meet Stanley Birt of the Legion. Mr Birt and I have met before – a big, cheerful-looking man, he is a former sergeant in the Coldstream Guards and now Deputy Secretary of the Services Department. When I get to the second floor he is already waiting – the Tribunal, he says, will begin in about ten minutes. We go to a small waiting room and he explains that this is one of seven tribunals which sit regularly in London and the main provincial cities. The case we are going to hear is that of Mr Jones – at least we will call him Mr Jones. An ex-R.A.F. corporal, he is now suffering from disseminated sclerosis. He is also one of the thousands who write to the Legion every year, asking help over pension problems.

Does every case, I ask, have to come before one of these tribunals?

Only if it's been put forward and turned down, says Mr Birt. 'When that happens a man has a right of appeal to an independent tribunal. The Legion takes up his case and our representative speaks for him.'

'So this isn't the first time the Legion has helped Mr Jones?'

By way of reply he indicates the dossier he carries. Two or three inches thick, it contains Jones's complete medical history, a mass of correspondence between Ministry and Legion. 'These are the papers dating from our original claim. Every time a man writes to us asking for help, we prepare his case and submit it for him. This is one of the cases that's been turned down. What happens this morning is called an Entitlement Tribunal.'

I ask if this happens in every case – or does the Legion sometimes accept the Ministry's verdict?

'We fight it in every case. If we don't we're prejudging the issue. Besides,' Mr Birt goes on, 'you never know what's going to come up – some point which may be of advantage to the man, that's somehow escaped everyone's notice. However hopeless a case might be, the Legion's got to fight it.'

There are still a lot more questions I want to ask, but now a brisk, efficient-looking young man joins us. This is Andy Thomas, the Legion's full-time representative at the tribunal. At thirty-six he is one of the Legion's new generation of officials – and one of four representatives who work at tribunals all over the country. After he has introduced us, Mr Birt asked Andy Thomas if Mr Jones is here yet.

'He's rolling a cigarette, poor chap. Feeling a bit nervous.' Andy Thomas goes back to look after Mr Jones: is his job, I ask, rather like being a defence counsel? Mr Birt considers this for a bit, then says not exactly, because nowadays the onus of proof is on the Ministry,

London like the back of your hand. George Stedman briefs five trainees from the Legion Taxi School.

Fund raising walks are an increasing branch activity. Charles Busby accompanies David Ennals, former Minister of State at the Ministry of Health and Social Security, and Mrs Ennals.

The original Poppy Factory in the Old Kent Road. Major George Howson, *front row centre*, with five original employees.

Today the Poppy Factory at Richmond employs 250 men. Talking to H.M. The Queen is John Trelford, formerly of the Durham Light Infantry.

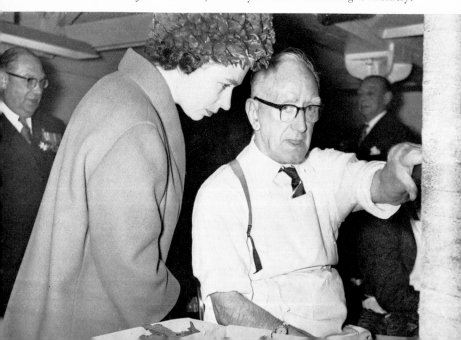

Earl Mountbatten, Grand President of the British Commonwealth Ex-Services League, greets member of the Nigerian Corps of Commissionnaires.

The League meets in Ottawa. On Earl Mountbatten's left, Canada's Minister for Veterans' Affairs, Roger Teillet.

For foreign visitors arriving at Gatwick, the Legion Courtesy Car can be their first introduction to Britain.

General Sir Charles Jones, the Legion President, greets some swinging poppy sellers in Chelsea.

The Prince of Wales tours the Cambrian Factory with the Chairman, Colonel Ralph Grimshaw.

Cambrian tweeds are sold at the Legion shop in Pall Mall along with deerstalker hats and dolls' deckchairs.

In 1946 Sir Winston Churchill presented Kippington Court, near Sevenoaks, to the Legion. He had been given the house by a wartime admirer. Now called Churchill Court, it is used as a convalescent home.

A branch meets beneath the motto 'Service not Self'. David Coffer, the present General Secretary is speaking.

Lister House, Ripon, is one of five residential homes which the Legion maintains for ex-servicemen.

Meanwhile the Housing Association has completed 615 flats, of which these at Howard Vyse Court, Clacton, are typical.

not the appellant. 'When a man comes before the tribunal they're in his favour,' he adds. 'We're reaping the rewards of the early pensions battles.'

By now it is almost time for the hearing to begin. We go down the passage to a large bright-looking room with Van Gogh reproductions and yellow curtains on the windows overlooking Store Street. The three members of the tribunal are already sitting: Sir Stafford Foster-Sutton, the Chairman, is in the middle. A large, amiable-looking man in a plum waistcoat, he is, says Mr Birt, a former Attorney-General of Malaya. Next to him sit the other members, one lay, one medical. The medical member is a high-powered consultant from the Royal Victoria Infirmary at Newcastle – because this morning's case is about multiple sclerosis, his special knowledge may be necessary. The lay member is Mr Powell, a former Legion Area Chairman. Sir Stafford says good morning and suggests we sit on the seats at the back. Apart from the Tribunal members and the clerk the only people present will be Mr Jones himself, Andy Thomas, and the Ministry representative.

A moment or so later these three file in. Mr Jones is in his forties: a tall, rather intellectual-looking man in a grey suit and white collar. He moves and talks with difficulty, but looks calm. Sir Stafford looks up and says good morning, he would like to put one or two points to him. The questions are probing but gently put. What the Tribunal have to decide, Mr Birt whispers, is whether the multiple sclerosis was brought on, or made worse by, Jones's time in the service.

'In January 1953 you started feeling unsteady on your legs?'

'Yes.'

'I just want to clear one or two things up. I don't suppose you remember it, Mr Jones, but you had a medical examination on release. You don't seem to have told them about this unsteadiness?'

'They didn't ask me about it.'

'They wouldn't have known to ask you, would they, unless they were told?' The hint of reproof is very mild; the whole atmosphere slow, sedate, informal. Sir Stafford pauses to make a note, then comes to a bit in the medical history where Mr Jones had a car accident. He wasn't really injured, says Mr Jones, he only had a black eye.

'I don't know,' says Sir Stafford. 'I'd call that a bit of an injury.'

He turns the pages of the file. In 1963, it seems, Mr Jones went absent without leave. Sir Stafford looks up, pained rather than disapproving. 'I wonder what made you do a thing like that? You seemed to be doing pretty well?'

Mr Jones says he supposes he lost his sense of responsibility. Was that, asks Sir Stafford, because he wasn't feeling well? Partly it was that, says Mr Jones – his balance and speech were getting worse. The Chairman glances at the other members of the Tribunal and sits back. 'I should think,' he says, 'that was the beginning of it.'

After this it is the Ministry's representative's turn. A courteous, quiet-voiced Scot, he has not much to add to the Ministry's original statement. He is followed by Andy Thomas who briefly goes over the case. 'I feel that on attributability I can't press with confidence. I'd like to submit on aggravation.'

There is a brief scratching of pens, then the Chairman

looks up. 'You really rely on the article don't you, Mr Thomas?'

Andy Thomas says he does, and Sir Stafford nods briefly. 'If you'll give us ten minutes to think this over,' he explains to Mr Jones, 'we'll let you know when we're ready.'

Mr Jones is helped out. What, I ask when we return to our waiting room, was all that about relying on the article?

'Article 4(2) of the Royal Warrant on Pensions,' explains Mr Birt. 'It says that a man can claim a pension even if his disability was not noted at his discharge, and was not the cause of his being discharged.' All this sounds rather complex to me, but Mr Birt is optimistic. He has been a tribunal representative himself, and clearly responds to the feeling of the courtroom. 'They'll give it on aggravation,' he says cheerfully. 'I'll be surprised if they don't.'

'If they do decide to give him a pension what will it be?'

'It'll be calculated as a percentage – part of the full disability pension of £8·40. The exact amount in each case is decided by the Ministry doctors,' he explains. 'If we think it's too little, we can write to them and argue. They may give in, or hold out.'

'Suppose they hold out?'

'Then we can take it to an Assessment Tribunal.' This, Mr Birt explains, sits in the same building and will also be attended by a Legion representative. The Legion's resources, it strikes me, are only matched by its patience – but meanwhile Andy Thomas comes back to say the Tribunal is ready. We file back into the room, where Mr Jones is already sitting.

The Chairman begins by reading the formal wording of the judgement. On the evidence before them, they say, the condition was pre-service and therefore not attributable. Under Article 4(2), however, the appeal is allowed.

When he has finished reading the rather ponderously-worded document, Sir Stafford turns to Mr Jones rapidly. I sense that he feels Mr Jones may have been baffled by the legal wording – he wants to let him know the result quickly. 'Now look here, we've allowed your appeal on aggravation. We don't think the Ministry have proved their case.'

'Right.' Mr Jones nods. It is his only reaction.

'You'll be hearing from the Ministry in due course. Now they'll get a taxi to take you back home.' Mr Thomas, it seems, has already arranged a taxi to Camberwell. This too, is part of the Legion's service.

Sir Stafford says good morning, and the clerk says he'll get Mr Jones's coat. It has not been a very dramatic morning in Store Street, but social services are not meant to be dramatic, they are meant to work. Society has done something to help Mr Jones. It has also affirmed a certain decency and fairness.

.   .   .   .   .

How much of what we have seen in Store Street is the result of the Legion's efforts?

In the earlier part of this book we saw how ceaselessly the Legion had worked in the 1920s to win a fair deal for the returning soldier. Better pensions and the compulsory principle in employing disabled men – these were the early battlegrounds. Even so, it was not till near the end of the Second World War that both principles were accepted. On pensions, since 1943, the onus of proof has been on the Ministry. Unless the Ministry could prove otherwise, it is now assumed, disability is due to a man's service.

Thus 1943 saw the greatest landmark in the story of pensions – but it was to be followed by anti-climax. As time went on it became increasingly clear that the new law was not working as Parliament had meant it. Often the Ministry continued to interpret the law in the old way – they went on placing the onus of proof on the man. Nor was the Legion's case helped by the fact that tribunals varied in their approach, or by the fact that it was still wartime. Indefatigable, the Legion battled to re-establish the principle which legally and morally it had already won. The Pensions staff undertook a crash programme of fighting what they knew were wrong decisions. In 1945 they were vindicated by a crucial judgement in the case of an appellant named Moxon. Moxon's appeal had gone from a tribunal to the High Court: Mr Justice Tucker said that the Ministry must produce a medical opinion to back their reasons for refusing a pension. This judgement was followed by many others between 1946 and 1948. Once the law had been thus established, the Ministry's attitude began to alter – from now on the law was administered as Parliament had meant it.

An additional help was the new Minister of Pensions in the Attlee Government of 1945 – the much-loved Clydesider Geordie Buchanan. 'He was the easiest I ever had to deal with,' recalls Sir Gordon Larking. 'I used to give him a pile of pensions claims, knowing he'd be fair about them, and ask him to use his own discretion.

' "Discretion," said Geordie, "I've got no discretion.

If you leave it to my discretion, I'll give every bugger a pension." '

Thanks to the Moxon judgement, the Legion had won – or rewon – its main battle. The theory was, as it should have been all along, put into practice. Meanwhile what was to happen to those who had unfairly been refused pensions in the intervening period?

Clearly, such cases could not go by the board. On the Legion's insistence, in 1946, the Ministry agreed to set up what were known as Special Review Tribunals. These had the power to reconsider all decisions that had been turned down during the interim. In the end, over forty per cent of all such adverse decisions were altered.

Meanwhile the key part of the 1943 Act had been the distinction between two articles – one of which we saw operating in the case of Mr Jones. Mr Jones's representative, you remember, let his case rest on Article 4(2). Under this a man could claim aggravation of a previously-existing illness – he could claim if his disability gave him trouble within seven years, even though it had not led to his being invalided. If a man was actually invalided from the service, on the other hand, he could claim under the other article 4(3). His disability had to be noted at the time of his discharge, and it had to be a cause of his being invalided. If both these conditions were met, then of course his case was a much stronger one.

The Legion had always accepted this distinction, but in 1965 there came a decision which interpreted the law more liberally. The Legion had appealed to the High Court in the case of a man named Judd, who had joined the R.A.S.C. in 1942 and suffered a severe fall during Selection Board exercises. Later he became ill with cervical spondylosis. The Legion claimed this was a result of his fall during service. Much complex medical and legal evidence was heard – finally Judge Edmund Davies not only decided in favour of Judd, but questioned the judgements in many previous cases. Some which had been previously decided under Article 4(2), his judgement implied, should have been given the same rights as they would have been under Article 4(3). It was an opportunity for the Legion which they seized with both hands: in consultation with the Ministry, they undertook a second massive review of all cases which could possibly be affected by the Edmund Davies decision. Where the Legion felt there was a real injustice, the Ministry agreed not to oppose them in the High Court. Today, six years after the Judd case, the Legion is still dealing with the backlog.

To the outsider the complexities of pensions law may seem abstruse, even pedantic. Yet what one cannot forget is the essential drive behind this immense, often tedious labour. Proper presentation of his case may make a difference of several pounds a week for a sick or disabled ex-soldier. With that in mind, no amount of litigation or paper work is too much for the Legion.

Often the Pensions staff has battled long and hard on a specific point, as it did in front of the McCorquodale Committee. Here it had been submitted that amputation meant more pain and disability as a man gets older – but the Legion wanted to improve the condition of *all* disabled pensioners, not only those who had lost their limbs during service. In the end the Legion succeeded in getting improved pensions for various degrees of amputation – and beyond it a new special allowance of £3 for all who were very severely disabled.

After the first war, only thirty per cent of men who

claimed pensions got them. After the second war, seventy per cent got them. That figure alone points the difference. Last year the Legion's Pensions staff dealt with just under 27,000 pensions queries: they represented ex-servicemen at 1,455 Entitlement Tribunals and just under 800 Assessment Tribunals. Since the Judd case they have dealt with 14,000 re-examinations, with another 2,000 still in the pipeline. Apart from this they have secured many more incidental benefits – the Constant Attendance Allowance for those who need someone to help them dress, and a Comforts Allowance of £1·25 a week for the badly disabled. Today around 6,000 war pensioners have a free car, plus a grant from the Ministry towards maintenance. Finally, over the years the basic pension rate has steadily risen – £1·63 in 1939, £4·88 in 1961, £8·40 in 1970.

In 1958 the Legion's Pensions Department was incorporated in the newly-formed Service Department. Its head, Major John Rivers, is a quiet, deceptively diffident man who now guides all Legion pensions strategy. Not infrequently the superficial diffidence goes – you will suddenly glimpse the depth of feeling he has for the ex-servicemen he speaks for. 'It's wrong that in a rich society like ours, the disabled should be made poorer by rising inflation. The basic pension today is worth a bit more than it was in 1938 – but not much. Because of this the fight for a higher basic rate has got to go on. It's as real a fight as it ever was.'

Today, unlike in the 1920s, it is fought from a position of strength. No other body in the country has such accumulated experience in pensions matters as the Legion: probably no area of the Legion's work has done so much to help ex-servicemen, or to improve the climate of public opinion. Dr Johnson once remarked that a society could be judged by the way it treated its old people. It might also be judged, he could have added, by its treatment of those who have fought and suffered for it.

12
The Roots are the Branches

THE British Legion was founded in 1921 – at the end of its first year there were 18,000 members. Today the figure is three-quarters of a million, spread over more than 4,000 local branches. If a local man has a pension problem or a soldier's widow wants to visit a war grave, then it is the branch who will write to headquarters. Each year over £200,000 from the central funds is allocated to the Service Committees of local branches, who in turn will use it for cases of hardship.

In one sense the branches are the roots – the life-blood of the British Legion.

．　　　．　　　．　　　．

The Bethnal Green branch meets in a room of a local Community Centre. On the walls are a poster for Poppy Day, certificates from the Legion Metropolitan Area, a dartboard. Most of the thirty or so men present are middle-aged – the atmosphere is hearty, comradely, classless. Before the meeting there have been a few army jokes, a bit of horseplay with someone imitating a bugle:

'That's not the Reveille, that's the bloody Retreat.' There is a general laugh, then the Committee take their places.

'Before we come to the evening's business, we've got two new members.' Mr Gable, the chairman, is a Civil Servant. He also seems to have the reputation of being a bit of a card – which does not mask the fact that for the last twenty years he has devoted most of his leisure to helping East End ex-service families.

The new members come forward and give their names. Both are second war men, one from the Sherwood Foresters.

'How's Robin Hood these days?' Mr Gable gives them both a cheerful welcome. 'Anyway we're glad to see you. Even if you have left it a bit late joining.'

When the new recruits sit down the atmosphere switches. We have come to the key moment of every branch meeting, the reading of the verse from Binyon's poem – as the Legion calls it, the Exhortation. At the far end of the room the standard-bearer raises the blue and gold standard and during the reading slowly dips it. Mr Gable speaks the words with resonance and feeling. When he comes to the end, the last line is repeated by everyone. 'We *will* remember them.'

It is less the reading of a poem than an affirmation – I am reminded of something that Arthur Markham, Chairman of the Legion Clubs Committee, has said about it. 'It's not a ritual, it's to set the scene. Whatever we're doing, we're doing it in the name of ex-servicemen who are no longer here. That's the motive spirit of the British Legion – that we're here because of the sacrifice of others.'

After the Exhortation we come to the minutes – one of this branch's special efforts is to send ten shillings and a birthday card to every old soldier in the Legion's residential homes on their birthdays. Mr Gable, it seems, has written a piece about this for one of the local papers. 'The *Hackney Gazette* murdered my article,' he says cheerfully, then sits back while the Secretary continues reading. The Mayor will be at Bethnal Green War Memorial on Remembrance Sunday, the band from a local school will provide five trumpeters. The new local M.P. has written accepting an invitation to be a Vice-President. The Legion branch at Arras is celebrating the anniversary of liberation – will the Bethnal Green branch sell some raffle tickets? 'We've got very strong links with them,' Mr Gable explains affably. 'Since we sent two old Somme men over last year for their anniversary. Treated 'em like royalty, they did.'

After the minutes the Pensions Secretary gets up. He stresses the importance of all pensions claims being put through the Legion. 'We've had a case this month of someone who put in their application themselves, and of course it got turned down by the Ministry.' Now the case will have to go to appeal, which the Pensions Secretary says need not have happened. 'They know how to put these things in Pall Mall. If you know anyone with a pension claim, tell 'em to come direct to the Legion.'

Besides being chairman, Mr Gable is also secretary of the branch Service Committee. Listening to its report, it is possible to wonder what happened to the social revolution – there must be thirty or forty people on the list all in need of something. An elderly man is permanently incapacitated – 'we'll be helping him with £15 for coal this winter'. One disabled man has not been out of his house for twenty-five years – the Legion is paying for him and his wife to go to a guest house at Brighton for a fortnight. An ex-serviceman had an accident at work – the branch has arranged for the Legion's solicitor to act for him at the hearing.

What seems to come out of the Service Committee's

report is not so much society's ingratitude or its brutality to the very poor, but its meanness. A court order has been made on an eighty-year-old man, and the Service Committee has to scrape around for a balance of £1.84 to help him. The branch got a new radio set for a home-bound widow, and now she's worried about having to pay for the licence. Another war widow has asked for help because her ceiling was damaged by flooding a year ago – Mr Gable has written twice to the G.L.C. who have promised help but done nothing. A small gift of pocket money has been made to an elderly couple who are getting a fortnight's holiday at a convalescent home.

'We like to do things a little better than the ordinary welfare,' says Mr Gable, and you can see what he means. What the Legion gives in Bethnal Green is not so much the money: it is the extra, unofficial touch of kindness.

.   .   .   .   .

Meanwhile what about the Legion's social side – the warming, cheerful sense of get-together which is why three-quarters of a million people join it?

In the four thousand Legion branches today this is not just the other side of the charitable coin, but part of it. When the social life thrives, mutual help is likely to be strongest. 'It's no good if what we do is just charity,' says Arthur Markham. 'It's got to be based on comradeship. Otherwise we might as well be civil servants.'

Is there a danger of such comradeship dying out – especially as new generations grow up to whom war is something that only happened in history? 'As seen from the outside,' wrote a village branch chairman in a recent issue of the *Journal*, 'the image of the village branch is not inspiring. It becomes increasingly to look like an old men's club, gradually dying out, with a backward-looking membership intent on the last war or the war before that, with little attention to give present conditions and less to the future.'

At the same time the view is widely held that there is less enthusiasm for ceremonial. 'The old chaps from World War One'll march,' said one branch chairman, 'but the trouble is they're getting past it. You ask a second war man to march – he'll tell you he did enough bloody marching in the army.'

They may not march, but they get together. The picture painted above may be true of many village branches, but there is another side to it. This is the steadily increasing strength of the club movement. Over the last seven years the number of clubs has gone up each year – today one branch in four has its own club premises, and a membership including wives and teenage children. At the Legion club at Hawkhurst in Kent, for instance, there is a membership of 500 from a population of 4,000. Few of the members here would ever go to the pub for the evening, in preference to the Legion club. The modern club-house has its own stage, bar, and billiard room. Every Saturday night there is a draw, with proceeds going to the Service Committee.

Often a Legion club can give a new life to a branch which has seemed in danger of losing heart – one example is the British Legion Club at High Openshaw, a district of Manchester now scheduled for massive redevelopment. Five years ago the Openshaw Legion branch was down to six members and £3 in the kitty. 'We used to meet in a room over a pub called the Wrexham,' says Charlie Gardner, the secretary. 'There were people in Openshaw who didn't know the Legion existed. Our Poppy Day takings were below £100. There was practically nothing in the way of social service.'

Largely as a result of Mr Gardner's enterprise, the Openshaw branch now has a membership of several hundred. He talked the St John Ambulance Brigade into selling them a bit of land cheap, got a loan from Whitbreads, and built a fine new club-house.

Today local teenagers flock to the club at week-ends; through the week there are the bars, bingo, and Wednesday night shows with professional entertainers. Poppy Day takings are more than quadrupled, thanks to efficient organization by the now flourishing Women's Section. 'Most important,' says Mr Gardner, 'the Legion has come alive again in Openshaw. A lot of old people have got around to realizing the Legion is there to help them. Ninety per cent of the pensions cases are people we've never heard of. Every other week we have a Service Meeting and it's surprising how many of the faces are new ones.'

Even so this scale of membership is small compared to some of the North's really booming clubs. At the new town of Newton Aycliffe, in County Durham, the membership is 1,650. For most of the 1,650 the British Legion Club is *the* social centre of the town. It has a restaurant and two bars, a concert hall, and a Wurlitzer. Every night of the week there is a special entertainment ranging from bingo to dancing and professional variety shows in the concert hall. In an average week, the treasurer reckons, the downstairs bar alone gets through £700 worth of brown ale. Apart from special nights for bingo and dancing you can belong to the Dicky Bow Club, whose members have to appear in something like two left shoes, and pay a forfeit if they fail to. Among more time-honoured local sports are the Pigeon Racing Club and the Leek Club, which recently paid out £800 in prizes for the best leek grown by a member. 'The record in this part of the country's 142 cubic inches,' says the secretary. 'Our first prize for the best leek's a bedroom suite.'

Part of this booming, bucolic success-story is linked to the fact that Newton Aycliffe itself is a new town. 'People moving in from other areas look around for a social centre,' says the secretary, George Shaw. 'They find the Legion.' Situated on the impressive concourse round the main civic square, the building is modern and eye-catching. The site was given by the town's Development Corporation to the Legion, who borrowed the money from Vaux's Brewery to put up the building.

The people who run the club are young – George Shaw is only thirty-six, and George Boyd, the chairman, was in the Navy till the 1950s. Because Newton Aycliffe is still expanding, the two Georges expect membership to double over the next few years. 'A lot of people come up here from the south of England,' says Shaw. 'They've never seen anything like this.'

For those who do move in from other parts of the country, talking about the service can be an introduction – George Boyd recalls being in the club one evening and meeting a new member who'd just moved up from London. 'We had a bit of a chat and it turned out we'd served together in the same ship, the *Battleaxe*. It's things like that that make the British Legion.'

Although the clubs accept some non-ex-service members, the proportion is strictly limited, both in numbers and to those who are genuinely in sympathy with the Legion's aims and interests. The success of Newton Aycliffe is never at the expense of Legion tradition. The Durham Light Infantry badge on the wall is there to inspire, not merely decorate: because this is the Legion, every dance or Saturday night variety show will end with the National Anthem. 'If anyone makes a move before the end they don't come back,' says George Shaw firmly. 'If they want to belong here, they do as we do.'

When an ex-serviceman dies in Newton Aycliffe, the branch will send a wreath of poppies. If the relations want, Ron Evans, the standard-bearer, will go to the funeral in his dark blue suit, beret, and sling, carrying the Legion standard. 'I lost a bit of work last year,' he says reflectively, 'twenty-four funerals.'

The point about a club like Newton Aycliffe is the extent to which it can underpin the branch's social service. Because of the club's scale and scope, the branch will get to hear that an ex-serviceman has died in the district. In the same way it will get to hear of a family in need, and because of its resources, it can help them. Any Newton Aycliffe couple going for a fortnight's holiday to one of the Legion's convalescent homes will get a gift of £5 pocket money. Recently the club gave £70 to the new Legion Housing Association flats at Bishop Auckland. Each year they give a Christmas dinner to old people, as well as taking four dozen bottles of ale for a party in a local old people's home. 'It's nothing to do with the Legion,' says George Boyd, 'but it's got a few ex-servicemen in it.'

Significantly, half the British Legion's total membership today is in one-quarter of the branches – those which have got club premises attached to them. 'Men and women are joining the Legion for a different reason,' says the Legion's General Secretary, David Coffer, 'from those for which their fathers joined. In the twenties there was so much to be put right – and they joined as a means of putting it right. Now they join for another reason – they want a social life, but with a purpose.'

13
Tweeds, Trays, and Tridents

PALL MALL is traditionally the heart of London's club-land – not the place where you would expect to find a doll's deck-chair or a deerstalker hat. But at Number 49, next to the Legion Headquarters, is the shop which sells all the products of its disabled workshops, from handbags to fine woollen ski-socks, Christmas crackers to clothes' airers and costume jewellery. Most come from Preston Hall and the Cambrian factory in Brecon. The smaller items are made by men working at home for another Legion-subsidized body, the Disabled Men's Industries.

Go down Pall Mall on a gloomy, rainswept day and let your eyes feast on the warm rich tweeds in the window, Lovat blue, green and tan, Donegall. Or better still go inside and buy a skirt length or a pair of superbly thick wool shooting stockings, £1·12 the pair. The grouse-moor may be out as a political image, but comfort isn't. Woollen ski socks come at 48p; a well-cut, made-to-measure skirt for £4·60, including the material. As a bargain it seems only beaten by the little Preston Hall plant-trough at 68p.*

Because more and more people want craftwork today, says Mrs Diana Barton who runs the shop, the demand for all these goods is growing steadily. She picks up a basket-edged tray, made by a disabled man from the New Forest. 'This man always sends us the most lovely things.' Mrs

* See page 51.

117

Barton knows most of the disabled workers herself, and goes to the Cambrian factory regularly. 'Though once you know them,' she adds, 'you don't think of them as disabled. You think of them as craftsmen.'

Recently Mrs Barton went to Heal's, who showed her a new Scandinavian travelling rug, designed in squares of orange and flame-colour. 'They suggested we might do something similar, so the Cambrian factory did.' The result was a series of brilliant new designs, pinks and mauves and blue pastels. Heal's took several dozen and more orders are on the way. The cheapest of the rugs sell at £1·65, and the most expensive at £3·30. 'The lifetime of a rug's supposed to be thirty years,' points out Mrs Barton. 'At that rate it's only ten new pence a year for the most expensive.'

·   ·   ·   ·

Even by the panoramic standards of Welsh roads, the A483 must be one of the loveliest. Leaving the market town of Builth Wells, it runs for several miles beside the rocks and waterfalls of the River Irfon. Presently it rises to higher ground and you get glimpses of the blue-misted hills of north Breconshire. Towns along the road are few – mostly it goes between fields and forests where the oaks have not yet been all replaced by pines. Half an hour's drive from Builth takes you to the next Wells, Llanwrtyd. It is pronounced, to English ears, *Clan-oor-tid*. As you approach the town, there is a large rectangular block on the right. This is the Legion's Cambrian factory.

The Cambrian factory has been producing fine Welsh textiles for more than half a century now. Originally a small hand-loom factory, it was given to the Legion by its owner, Mr Arthur Beckwith, in 1927. Today it employs forty-two disabled people and produces 50,000 yards of fine Welsh tweed a year – the products we have already seen in Pall Mall, and which are also on sale in the small cream-painted shop which adjoins the factory.

Even on an autumn day there are several holidaymakers' cars parked outside. The A483 is a main route from the North-West to Swansea and the South Wales resorts. 'When I first came here,' says Jack Jones, the ex-gunner who runs the shop, 'it used to be a quiet road. Now the season goes on all the year round. On a good day in the summer, we'll take between £100 and £200.'

Ten years ago the total sales of the factory were £18,000; in 1970, the figure was more than trebled. 'The Welsh textile industry still remains faithful to wool,' says Eric Hetherington, the factory manager. 'We use only Welsh wool here, from the Radnor breed of sheep.' Many of the products are sold through branches of the Women's Section, but because the factory's high quality products appeal especially to overseas buyers, the export trade with America and Australia is increasing.

Recent exhibitions include one at the London Hilton, and among Mr Hetherington's newest successful markets are the Officers' Wives' Clubs attached to American bases in Britain. 'It's not only the end-product we sell,' he points out, 'it's the follow up. If we sell one skirt-length in an Officers' Wives' Club in Ruislip, we may get ten orders back from the U.S.A. When we sell it's because we make good tweed – not because the chap who made it's got a leg off.'

Eric Hetherington knows about good tweed. He grew up in the woollen trade in Yorkshire – before the war he was a bobbin-boy, handling yarn. When he came out of the R.A.F. he went on to weaving, then to night school to learn textile designing. 'After that I went to one of the big mills,' he recalls, 'and they asked me what I'd done. I told them, and in the end they gave me a job. "We've had a lot of better men than thee," they told me, "but thou'rt cheapest." '

When it comes to selling the Cambrian factory's goods, Eric Hetherington still applies the same tough Yorkshire standards. The other half of his job is to know and understand the needs of all his workpeople. If any has a problem they knock on his door; if a man who's on pills has to go to the dentist, Mr Hetherington reminds him to take an extra tablet in case he finds the visit stressful.

'This is the cream of the job,' he says, 'that I'm here to help people, even if I only smile at them or have a word when I'm going round. One day when I was going round the mill a little man stopped me. "I want to thank you for smiling at me," he said, "you don't know what it means to be noticed." Somebody says something like that, it cuts you down to size. It's the hardest thing for a disabled man – the feeling of not being wanted.'

Unlike other Legion workshops, the Cambrian factory employs a relatively high proportion of non-ex-service disabled people. At the moment the number is about half. These include local blind people, spastics, and epileptics, whose training and disability grants are paid by the local authority. 'In years to come,' thinks Mr Hetherington, 'this new need will become greater.' He tells me about one case he recently took on, of a young man suffering from spinal byfida. 'Until recently, no one survived from the disease. This boy's one of the first generation to live. As time goes on there'll be more like him, and they'll need to find employment in factories like this one.'

Because the factory is so geographically isolated, it has to be a completely self-contained unit. Mr Hetherington's own house is next door to the shop. Most of the work people live in two groups of houses close by, and the single men in a hostel in the village.

The factory has its own Social Club with bingo, film shows, and concerts. One of the most active on the social committee is Bryn Jones, the factory foreman and son of a first war serviceman. He grew up in one of the houses here, and now helps run the social club, Llanwrtyd's fire brigade and also the local branch of the Legion. 'Some people ask what we find to do in the country,' he says. 'I wonder what they find to do in the town.'

As we go round the factory Eric Hetherington explains the complex process of weaving. We talk to Owen who stirs the fleeces in the dye-vat – it seems hard to imagine that the black, vinegar-smelling, soaking mass can ever achieve the heathery textures of Lovat. 'Hallo Idris, hallo Jack.' Between introductions we pause to look at the new machines. Currently the factory is introducing new automated methods, which will not only make for easier working conditions, but also for more production and tighter quality control.

Upstairs in the weavingroom there is a small group of visitors going round – a group of late holiday-makers who have stopped at the shop and are now on a tour of the factory. We stay with them to admire the subtle green and orange of a new yarn, then go over to talk to David, a young blind man who works on one of the weft-winding machines.

David has been here eight years, he tells me; before that he'd never been able to settle to anything. The machine he operates looks difficult for anyone who can see, let alone a blind man. David was determined to succeed, and completed the six months' training in three months.

The other point is involvement, Mr Hetherington adds – David works as part of a team, with others.

'It's better than making a basket,' he says as I watch David working. 'A basket's a world of your own.'

David agrees. 'I wanted to do it as fast as anyone that could see. Then no one could say I was holding the team back.'

I ask if it isn't difficult to find his way round the complicated bobbins and spindles, and David grins. 'Where you'd use your eyes, I just know where to put my hands down.'

In a sense I feel David is a symbol of what the Cambrian factory is trying to do. I say so to Mr Hetherington as we go down the stairs into the autumn sunshine.

'The point with disabled people is to make a contact, a sharing of interest,' he says. 'That's what I'd like to think we're doing.'

I get into the car and drive off. Soon the factory, the shop and the houses are small dots against the grandeur of the Brecon mountains. Even against such a background there seems something permanent about the little cluster of buildings: part of a continuing tradition of service, inspired by the Legion's caring.

.   .   .   .   .

Car parks might sound depressingly urban after the Brecon hills. Yet these are another important facet of the industry which the Legion sponsors. The British Legion Attendants Company is not merely a thriving business. It provides work for an increasing number of men, and calls for above average efficiency and responsibility.

Basically the Attendants Company operates car parks on behalf of local authorities. Its uniformed attendants collect the fees for them: they themselves are paid by the Company, out of an agreed charge made to the local authority. 'It's now the most widespread and economical car parking organization in the country,' says Arthur Markham, Chairman of the Attendants Company. 'In cities and towns, on new permanent sites or on temporary car parks, our attendants see that all cars are parked in an orderly way, and keep the necessary records.'

Mr Markham believes the success of the scheme depends on public confidence in a man in uniform. Some of the attendants are partially disabled, though not to the degree that would make them candidates for a disabled workshop. All wear the company's distinctive dress, blue uniform, white peaked cap, and a British Legion flash on the shoulder. The work is not just in car parks – Legion attendants work as commissionaires, security officers, and telephone orderlies. You can see them at Wimbledon, Olympia, the Royal Tournament, the National Eisteddfod, and most of the London art galleries. When one woman demonstrated her dislike of a picture in a recent Royal Academy exhibition by sticking her umbrella through it, it was a Legion attendant who gently but firmly restrained her.

Unlike the disabled workshops, the company does not take any subsidy from central Legion funds – in fact it makes a healthy and increasing profit. The latest figures show a trading surplus of close on £30,000 – nearly half as much again as the previous year. The company makes an annual donation of £1,500 to Legion benevolent funds, and has invested a further £30,000 in the Housing Association. The numbers of men employed, too, are going up: in

1970 the company paid out just on half a million pounds in wages.

Building on this success-story, the Attendants Company is today looking forward. There is the new airports division, managing the parking facilities at Gatwick and Stansted. Mr Markham also has plans for a quite new venture, for special guards to look after high-security lorry compounds. 'This is something the Ministry of Transport have asked local authorities to set up,' he says. 'We hope to open the first one at Preston shortly.' He explains that lorry drivers need a night's sleep on long journeys, and they can't get it if they've left the lorry with a valuable load just parked outside a transport café. Under Mr Markham's scheme the driver would bring his lorry into a specially-wired and patrolled compound, hand it over to a Legion guard, then go off to have a meal and a night's sleep. 'This not only makes sense as a public service,' says Mr Markham. 'Through the Attendants Company we can provide the right kind of men to handle it.'

In fact the blueprint for such a plan already exists – in the special scheme run by the Airports Division at Gatwick Airport.

. . . . .

'At the rate this airport's expanding, we'll soon be parking a couple of million cars a year.' George Morley looks up, as yet another Trident roars off the runway. As manager of the Legion Attendants at Gatwick he is responsible for employing fifty men. By 1972, he reckons, there will be a need for three times that many.

At Gatwick, he explains, the problems are not simply looking after car parks. There *are* ordinary parks where you can leave your car for a couple of hours – but there are also special ones for people leaving their cars for a weekend, or while they're in, say, Majorca for a fortnight.

The twenty-five men in charge of the ordinary parks are mostly the older ones. The other half of the staff are dog-handlers, security men, and drivers. All attendants wear the special Airports Division dress – beret, tie, and battledress with a British Legion flash on the shoulder. 'It's not a bad advertisement, come to think of it,' says George Morley. 'The Legion uniform's the first thing a lot of people see when they come to England.'

After we have looked at one of the ordinary parks he suggests I might like to take a look at the special ones for long-term parking. With his assistant, Dennis Jeans, I get into a brightly painted green Ford van labelled 'Courtesy Car. British Legion Attendants'.

'What's the idea of the Courtesy Car?'

'We try to make people feel we look after them. They leave their own cars in the ordinary park, then the Courtesy Car takes them to the Arrival Building.'

'So what happens to their own car meanwhile?'

'Let's say it's a man going to Italy for a fortnight. We get him to agree the petrol and speedo reading, hand over the keys, and make a note of any valuables. The next stage is where our own drivers come in – one of them'll take the car over to the Beehive. That's where it stays till he comes back.'

'What's the Beehive?'

'The old Control Tower.' Dennis Jeans points to a round, squat building which I remember seeing from the Brighton trains in the thirties – the Beehive is not ill-named. Today it stands between the helicopter park and some slightly rusting green hangars. This is the original

Gatwick aerodrome, away from the perimeter of the modern airport. Close to the Beehive, Mr Jeans points to a wired fence, where another man in Legion blue is putting a guard dog through its paces.

We get out of the Courtesy Car and he introduces me to Terry Barber, the dog-handler, who in turn introduces me to his Alsatian, Champ. Champ goes home with him and plays with his two children, he says – he's never yet had to let him loose on anyone. 'If you do get anyone inside the park, it's usually a few skinheads or a courting couple. We don't set the dog on them, we just call out. "Stop. I have a dog with me." It does stop them too, I can tell you.'

As we drive back to the perimeter Dennis Jeans points out two other huge long-term car parks. 'If you came in the summer, you'd see them packed, all ten acres. That means each of our drivers is shifting eighty cars a day – forty when the owner leaves them, forty when he comes back.'

What, I ask, are the problems in driving eighty different cars in a day – including foreign ones? Dennis Jeans, who learned his own driving in the R.A.S.C. in World War Two, says he's known some funny ones. 'The worst are the ones where they've got burglar alarms, and leave you to find out about them. You get all sorts here, Rolls, Minis, and a few old bangers. We have conferences over a few, but mostly if a driver doesn't know the gearbox or the starting mechanism, someone else will.'

Even so, he adds, driving ability is not the only thing. More important still is responsibility. Since the Legion took over Gatwick has never had a case of pilfering, and they've never had to sack anyone.

'Because it's the Legion,' says Mr Jeans, 'people trust us. That's something to live up to.'

14
The Continuing Debt

PICTURES from some of the Legion's country homes: still
sprightly in his late sixties, Nobby Clark joined up in the
first war as a boy bugler. He used to box a bit in the old
days, then got his teeth knocked out. 'So I had to give up
bugling. I'm still the harmonica player here, but I have
to take my teeth out ... I like it here, I've been in worse
stations. Main fact is, I have to wear these calipers and
they're a strain on my heart. They used to say I hadn't
got a heart, I'd got a swinging brick. That's when I was a
sergeant in The Wiltshires ...'

Some very old soldiers have a jauntiness about them,
almost like schoolboys. In another country home a trim
old man of nearly ninety: he shows me some press cuttings
about himself and his brother, both from the Boer War,
and then I ask if he has any hobbies.

He draws himself erect, almost saluting. 'Whisky,
sir.'

Afterwards I ask the Warden if he really gets any, and
the Warden grins. 'He's getting a bit past it these days, but
he'll go to the pub when he can.

'There's always someone to buy him a pint of bitter and
listen to his stories. If he has one too many, they'll put
him in a taxi and pay for it. They'll always see him home
safely ...'

Old soldiers, they say, fade away. In the Legion homes
they can do so with dignity, old comrades round them,

kindness. For many thousands of others the picture is less comforting; anyone who thinks poverty has been abolished in Britain should take a quick look at the records of the Legion's Service Department. Half-ton coal allowances for the permanently incapacitated, country holidays for the severely disabled – even down to finding the bus fares. One might suppose these were the days of Jarrow, not the affluent society.

The Service Department spends three-quarters of a million pounds annually to meet the most urgent of these human needs. The man who does the dispensing is Major John Rivers. Quickly he ticks off the items – nearly £200,000 paid out through the branches, to help local cases of hardship. £54,000 on residential homes; another £50,000 for the convalescent homes where elderly couples can get a fortnight's holiday. (At, for example, such places as Churchill Court, Sevenoaks, which Sir Winston gave to the Legion in 1946.) One of the largest items is the £230,000 for the permanently incapacitated or their widows. This is paid in the form of a 50p a week extra pension, and goes mostly to first war survivors in real need. 'A sixth of them go to Southern Ireland,' says Major Rivers, 'where the level of public assistance is very low. You get the widow of someone who served with the Irish Guards – in some of the rural areas, these people are living on the tea and bread level.'

Beyond this the Department can give loans and small advances in cases where someone is desperate. There may be the occasional scrounger but in general Major Rivers prefers to give people the benefit of the doubt. 'Sometimes you have to take a chance,' he says. 'If in doubt I'd always rather help a scallywag than turn down a good person.' Recently he went to see an old man who was gassed at

Arras, and didn't apply for a pension in 1919 because he didn't want to be a burden on his country. 'Now he's old and infirm and poor,' says Rivers, 'and he badly needs a pension. The country won't give him one because he ought to have applied before, and in any case all the papers have been destroyed long ago. As I came away, I thought, he did all that for his country. Now the country says there's no proof, no contemporary records – so he can't have a pension. If he'd been a World War II man all this would have been different – but it seems a poor lookout. He fought and he risked his life, all for a bob a day. Now the country can't do anything to help him.'

The continuing need remains. Another way the Legion helps to meet it is through the Women's Section, which now has nearly 3,000 branches up and down the country. In most it is not only a social service, but a focus for the life of small communities. 'If anyone needs help in this village,' to quote one Norfolk teenager, 'it's the British Legion Women's Section that helps them. Apart from that they keep the social life going. If it wasn't for them, there'd be hardly anything going on in most of the villages round here.'

Village entertainments, coffee mornings, and bring-and-buy sales may seem the small change of welfare work, but it is in such ways that the Women's Section gets the funds for an impressive record of service. The Section has its own Welfare Fund, and runs rest homes at Weymouth and Bridlington. Shortly it will open three new blocks of flatlets for ex-service women and widows.

Since 1939 it has also had its own Widows' Allowance system which pays 63p a week to nearly 500 widows, three-quarters of them in the Irish Republic. Nor is it simply a question of raising money and spending it. What really counts, says Mrs Croft Foulds, the National Chairman, is the sense of personal dedication. 'In one hospital near Leeds,' she says, 'there are still paraplegic cases from World War I. I know one woman who's gone there for the last twenty years. She's baked cakes and taken them in on a Saturday and fed the men herself, and done their shopping and sewing for them.'

Much of this service is for the very old, but not all of it. For the next few years the Women's Section will be helping a small Maltese boy to play football. 'The boy's father was a sergeant in the Army who died,' says Mrs Croft Foulds. 'There was no pension, and the widow has only three pounds a week to keep three children. The boy had passed the exam to go to a grammar school, but his mother couldn't afford to let him because of the extras. We heard of the case and decided to pay for the things he needed, like clothes and pocket money and football boots – the money's paid through the Malta branch in two lots of £30 a year. It doesn't seem all that much, but to that one little boy it'll make a difference.'

Across the hills from the Cambrian Factory lies the small country town of Bwlch, in the Usk valley. To this valley, long ago, there came the second Roman legion who fought near Bwlch, at a place whose Welsh name means the Valley of the Slaughter. Today Bwlch is the home of Legionaries of another kind – the fifty-six old soldiers who live at Crosfield House, just outside it.

Crosfield House is one of five country houses which the Legion maintains as a permanent home for aged or infirm ex-servicemen. All are supervised by nursing staff, but their aim is to provide something more than just medical care. In a real sense Crosfield House and the others like it are homes, with the accent on comradeship and friendship.

The present Crosfield House was built at the turn of the century. Beyond its yew-hedges and parkland, it looks to the Brecon mountains. The house itself suggests solidity and warmth – there are oak panels, heavy doors, bright furnishings. The enormous Hall downstairs is the main sitting-room. It has billiards, goldfish tanks, and superb views over the park and meadows. Perhaps twenty or thirty men sit around in small groups, talking or watching television. The atmosphere is that of a club, relaxed, un-institutional. 'If you make too many rules,' says Mr Toomey, the Secretary, 'someone'll break them. If a man wants to go to bed early and listen to *The Archers* in his bedroom, then he can do. Another man'll sit up reading till half past ten. We don't make them do anything.'

Although there are separate rooms, most men sleep in small dormitories: if one man has an accident, says Mr Toomey, then the others can help him. 'Six years ago an old man had a bad fall and fractured his hip,' he recalls, 'and we got him to hospital within fifteen minutes. If he'd been on his own, he might have stayed there hours with no one to help him.'

What sort of man comes to Crosfield House? Two-thirds of the fifty-six, says Mr Toomey, are First World War men; if they hadn't been able to come here, they'd be in geriatric hospitals. 'Or sometimes you'll get a younger man, where the wife walks out. We had one fifty-year-old man with a coronary. It left him paralysed on one side – his wife couldn't stand it and left him. You may say it's wrong, though I wouldn't judge anyone. All the same, that's the kind of need we're here for.'

Crosfield House cannot stop life being hard. What it can do is to give people hope, and a sense of belonging. As you walk round, the sense of belonging is evident –

a little group playing cards, one old man helping another one into supper. When one patient won £400 on the pools, he gave a £100 for extra comforts for the others. Another man left to go and live with relations in the Midlands, who'd built an annexe on to their house for him; he came back within a fortnight. 'Partly I think he was afraid it wouldn't work,' says Mr Toomey, 'but the other thing was that he missed everyone. Here he had his talk, and his friends, and his dominoes.'

Although it is so deep in the country, there is no feeling of isolation at Crosfield House. Relations come to visit; three times a week a party goes into Brecon on the special mini-bus. 'All the local people are kind,' says Mr Toomey, 'if they see one of the old boys out walking and he looks a bit tired, they'll give him a lift home. It's one of the advantages of a small community – everybody knows them.' In the evenings there may be a visit from a choir from one of the mining valleys nearby. Among other friends are the Ebbw Vale Rotary Club, who every summer take a party in their own cars to a county match at Swansea, where they have lunch in the pavilion with the cricketers.

Above all at Crosfield House there is talk, talk of days gone by, the pleasure of very old men exchanging memories. Bangalore, the Boer War, Salonika – in the big sitting-room the names weave in and out of the conversation like scrolls on some faded battle-honours. 'Finest body of men I've ever seen,' says one man, 'the Bengal Lancers. When they lost their lances, out'd come their swords.' As I leave the evening's television-viewing is about to begin; the chairs are drawn up, the cups of cocoa marshalled. 'Show-jumping,' says an old cavalryman, 'I like that. When they get up to seven-foot-two.'

I say goodnight, and go out into the cool Welsh evening. If the Legion had no other reason to exist, it seems to me, Crosfield House would be one.

15
Into the Future

Miss Linda Millward comes from Gloucestershire. During the war she was an A.T.S. sergeant, attached to an ack-ack regiment. Afterwards she worked in Brighton for the Ministry of Social Security, became ill, and had to retire two years before she should have got her pension.

At this time Miss Millward was living in one room at the top of eight flights of stairs. This had been all right when she was still working, but after she was ill she could no longer manage them. She put her name down for a council flat, and for two years nothing happened. One day she was talking to a friend about what she should do, and the friend came up with an idea. Why didn't Miss Millward write to the British Legion? They might have some sort of housing scheme for ex-service people. If not, they might at least be able to help her or advise in some way.

The answer was that the British Legion could, and did, help Miss Millward. Today she lives in a first-floor flat at Howard Vyse Court, a modern architect-designed estate at Clacton. From picture windows she has a view over fields and beech trees. The flat itself has two rooms with a labour-saving kitchen, concealed central heating, and a grey-tiled bathroom, for all of which she pays five pounds a week, including electricity. If Miss Millward wants to join in any activities, there is a communal room where tenants meet for social evenings and coffee mornings. Should she need anything or be taken ill, there is a warden who will come round at the press of a buzzer.

Howard Vyse Court is one of nine schemes now completed by the Legion Housing Association. Working through Government subsidies and in close co-operation with local authorities, the Association has already passed its Jubilee year target – 1,000 flats where elderly couples or single ex-service people can spend their later years in security and comfort. The scheme not only takes the pressure off local housing lists. For many, it means all the difference between a real home and an institution.

'A lot of places are taken up in old people's homes by people who don't really need to be there,' says John Rivers. 'What so many older people need is just someone to keep an eye on them. This is why each housing scheme has a warden and his wife, whose job is just to be there.' If an old lady at Howard Vyse Court wants an electric lamp fixed, Mr King, the warden, will do it for her. If a new couple move in, his wife will provide cups of tea and generally help them. 'If we don't see somebody about for a couple of days,' says Mr King, 'we'll go and make sure they're all right. Otherwise we don't trouble them. As I see it, we're a sort of lifeline.'

A sort of lifeline – the words could stand as a modest summary of the Legion's half-century of service. The Housing Association is only the most recent link in the chain – disabled industries, residential homes, local branch work, disability pensions. Since 1921, the Legion has spent forty-three million pounds on various forms of welfare. In pensions and securing employment for the disabled, it has been a formidable pressure group. Over the whole range of ex-servicemen's welfare, it would not be too much to say the Legion has transformed the social conscience of the nation.

.   .   .   .   .

Where, in a world it has so greatly helped to change, does the Legion go next?

Dennis Cadman, the National Chairman since 1968, believes it can be more, not less effective in the 1970s. At forty-eight he is one of the second war generation who today are guiding the Legion's future. When he came out of the Army, he joined his local branch in Essex, and has ever since taken an active interest in all forms of the Legion's social service. 'I suppose I feel grateful for coming out of the war whole myself,' he says. 'Working for the Legion's a way of saying thank-you.' Each month he travels hundreds of miles, addressing meetings and holding press conferences, particularly outside London. 'I wouldn't say we're trying to promote the Legion's image,' he says, 'because I don't think image is the right word. What we are trying to do is give people a better understanding of our aims. Nowadays we're getting far more notice in the press. New projects like the Housing Association are bringing the Legion's name before the public.'

Mr Cadman would like to see a Legion branch at the centre of each community; he gives as an example a recent case where a new road was needed to give access to an old peoples home. 'There was nobody else around to do the job, so the local Legion branch did it.' In this kind of way the Legion is ideally suited for all-purpose social service; among other new projects, Mr Cadman is enthusiastic about one to provide Outward Bound courses for the sons of ex-servicemen. 'We in the Legion have faith in young people,' he says. 'We wanted to show we had this faith – a positive recognition of our belief in them.'

Mr Cadman also stresses the increasing contact with overseas ex-servicemen. He chairs the working party of the Commonwealth Ex-Services League, which has recently sent tractors and equipment to a farm for ex-servicemen in Ceylon, and given £10,000 to help Indian ex-soldiers. It sent £5,000 to help the Gurkha fund and in other ways has helped servicemen throughout Africa, Asia, and the Caribbean. 'Seventeen and a half million men from the Commonwealth helped us in our hour of need,' says Mr Cadman. 'Now many of them are in need – and it's our turn to help them.'

Although Dennis Cadman looks forward to new ideas, he thinks the Legion could not survive if it became merely another organization for social service: it would be wrong for it to change its identity as a primarily ex-service body.

If there are no more major wars, does this mean the Legion's future might not extend beyond the end of the century? Mr Cadman accepts the possibility, but at the same time points out that huge numbers of World War Two men will need increasing help as they reach their sixties and seventies.

The other point is that new vitality can come from younger men leaving the forces. 'For them, the Legion can be not only a social life but a challenge,' says Mr Cadman. 'It'll be our fault if they don't join because they haven't been told sufficiently what it's all about.'

Clearly the future may mean changes, but Mr Cadman stresses that the Legion as a body is well used to adapting itself – as the state develops new welfare services, for example, it may need to switch its own resources elsewhere. 'The point is that the resources are there to help those in need, and will be for the foreseeable future. Meanwhile the Legion is accustomed to change – not afraid of it.'

Whatever changes the 1970s bring, David Coffer, the General Secretary, is likely to be the man responsible for guiding the Legion through them. Recently he completed a two months' tour giving advice to ex-service organizations in India, Nepal, Ceylon, and Pakistan. Among his travels nearer home have been thirty-mile fund-raising walks over the North Downs, where he has led groups including teenagers and Government ministers to raise extra funds for Poppy Day.

As General Secretary, he sees his job as essentially to reconcile views that may widely differ. 'The Legion,' he says, 'is an infinitely democratic body. Any important change has to work its way up from the branches, and be debated on the floor of our annual Conference. This has always been the strength of the Legion – the justification of our claim to speak for the whole ex-service movement.'

In the immediate future the controversial issue is likely to be that of membership. At the moment a British Legion club can take up to forty per cent of non-ex-servicemen, or thirty per cent if the branch has no Women's Section. Daughters of ex-servicemen may join but not, paradoxically, sons. One school of thought would like to see these rules broadened and relaxed. As the older generation dies off, they say, this would not only mean a continuity of membership – it would mean opportunities for new and different forms of social service.

This is one view of the membership question – the other is that such a broadening would reduce the whole point of the Legion. Only by keeping the ex-service principle at the centre, say the supporters of the second view, can the Legion hope to keep the character and influence built up over half a century.

Whichever view prevails, David Coffer believes that membership itself is not the whole point: above all, the aim must be to help ex-servicemen. Over the years, he points out, the Legion has evolved a vast organization for doing good. Increasingly this can now help a wider public – through the club movement, through disabled workshops, like Preston Hall and the Cambrian Factory. 'But I believe we must always keep the organization separate from the fund-raising. That must be for the ex-servicemen and women. It may be the Second World War man who will need help twenty-five years from now. It may be the soldier who gets shot in Belfast tomorrow. The point is that the Legion is there to help.'

After fifty years, it remains the continuing purpose.

·   ·   ·   ·   ·

The new Legion President, General Sir Charles Jones, is also a second war man. The first of Haig's successors who was too young for the first war, he fought at Dunkirk, Nijmegen, and was later Chief of Staff to the 14th Army. Since 1969 he has been Governor of the Royal Hospital, Chelsea. Appropriately, my last Legion visit is to see him at the great Wren building which Charles II began for his old soldiers three hundred years ago.

I go to the gate where there is one of the blue-coated old soldiers sitting and say I have an appointment with Sir Charles Jones.

'You mean General Jones.' The very old man glances at me tolerantly, then directs me to the Governor's office. I wait for a moment in the hall where there are paintings of Waterloo, the long oak table where Wellington lay in state. Here I am greeted by Sir Charles, and by his Jack Russell terrier who presently subsides in a corner of his office.

Sir Charles fills his pipe slowly while he talks. He is clearly a man of range, of thought as well as action. I begin by asking him if he feels his Presidency will be different because he comes from a younger generation.

'I suppose one looks at it differently in this way. There was much more horror attached to World War I. Even allowing for the destruction of somewhere like Coventry or Hamburg, it was never quite as bad. You never got anything like the Somme, where 50,000 men were mown down between dawn and mid-day. In this way, naturally, one does look at it differently. But the aims of the British Legion – its beliefs – there's no change there.'

Does he feel, I ask, that the Legion's aims and activities are getting across to the wider public?

'I think they're getting across much better now. Even so, a lot of people still think of us as a sort of old comrades' association, a lot of jollification and beer-drinking. Not enough people know the real work that goes on – for instance the pensions and welfare work, or new things like the Housing Association.'

Will these new activities, I ask, mean a shift of emphasis – as the Legion begin to develop new kinds of projects, will there be less stress on some of the older ones.

'I think we've got to be prepared for change.' Sir Charles considers for a moment, glancing through the window at the winter sunlight as it glows on the red brick of the great courtyard. 'Some of the activities which have been good in the past, may not be so relevant in the future. You take something like the Cambrian Factory which has been serving disabled people for fifty years. There might come a time when we should say that it's done its work for ex-servicemen – that it'd be more use as part of the wider social services. If that did happen, then I think we in the Legion should feel proud rather than sorry. We'd have done the pioneering work and blazed a trail – in that as in so many other ways.'

One way he would like to spread the Legion's name is by encouraging new kinds of youth activity. 'You take a Legion branch, say in some outlying part of the country. Suppose the branch sets itself to organize a small group of young people – it needn't be a lot of them, but a small hard core, who feel a genuine idealism. They might devote themselves to looking after the dependents of ex-service people, reading to them, helping them, visiting. In time that could easily widen out beyond the purely ex-service community, to looking after all the old and infirm in a district. If something like that happened in one branch, it could happen in others. It could spread.'

We talk a little longer, then Sir Charles asks if I would like to have a look at the rest of the Hospital. We go across to the main courtyard, his Jack Russell scouring the perimeters as the old soldiers go into lunch. There are about four hundred of them now, Sir Charles tells me, including twenty-five who go back to the Boer War. We look into the Great Hall, the faded campaign flags from Waterloo, the old leather gallon-jugs on the oak table. He stops to talk to some of the old men; as we come out again into the courtyard he tells me how Wren not only built the place but helped to plan its organization. 'Most of it still runs pretty smoothly today,' he says. 'The twentieth century hasn't improved on it much.'

As we cross the courtyard he pauses to read the Latin

inscription over the Colonnade. 'For the help and happiness of those of merit, broken by age or war,' he translates. 'Started by Charles the Second.'

'In its day it was a sort of British Legion?'

'The sort of thing that the Legion would have inspired, yes. Almost a sort of forerunner.' He pauses. 'I think of it this way – you've got this organization, devised three hundred years ago, persisting to this day, and still being considered good and up-to-date.'

I make a note of Sir Charles' words and repeat them. 'Devised three hundred years ago, persisting to this day—'

'And still being considered good,' says Sir Charles. 'That's the real point. I'd like to think people might say the same of us, some time in the future.'

Index